Hope this one is small enough to carry! Enjoy! CW 12/99

S0-ABQ-958

the JAPANESE
TRAVELMATE

Compiled by Lexus
with Helmut Morsbach
and Kazue Kurebayashi

Chronicle Books · San Francisco

First published in the United States in 1991 by
Chronicle Books.

Printed in the United States of America.

Cover design: Kathy Warinner
Composition: TBH Typecast

ISBN: 0-87701-875-8

10 9 8 7 6 5 4 3 2 1

Chronicle Books
275 Fifth Street
San Francisco, California 94103

 printed on recycled paper

YOUR TRAVELMATE

gives you one single easy-to-use list of useful words and phrases to help you communicate in Japanese. Built into this list are:

–Travel Tips with facts and figures that provide valuable information

–typical replies to things you might want to say.

On pages 119–126 there's a list of Japanese characters as seen on signs and notices. A menu reader is given on pages 62–72 and numbers on pages 127–128. Translations are written in a modified form of the standard Hepburn romanization of Japanese (romaji).

Some notes on pronunciation

a   as in "father"
e   as in "bet"
i   as in "Maria" or "pier"
o   as in "modern"
u   as in "put"

For double vowels give each its value as above:

ai   as in "Thailand"
ae   pronounced "ah-eh"
ei   as in "weight"
ie   pronounced "ee-eh"
ue   pronounced "oo-eh"

When there is a bar over a vowel this means that you should give it twice the length, for example: "chizu" (map) but "chīzu" (cheese). A bar over an "o" gives it a sound as in "paw."

g   as in "gift"
r   between English "r" and "l" (there's no "l" in Japanese); the tip of the tongue hits the ridge above your front teeth
s   as in "glass"
y   always as in "yes," never as in "by"

A final "e" is always a separate sound; so "kare" (he) is pronounced "ka-reh" and not as English "care." Think of the pronunciation of "karate."

(no), (na)

These words are used in front of a noun: "kara no heya" (an empty room). But after a noun they are omitted: "heya wa kara des" (the room is empty).

....

a, an *Japanese has no word for "a"*
abacus soroban
abdomen hara
about: about 15 jugo kurai
  about 2 o'clock niji goro
above ... ... no ue ni
abroad kaigai ni
absolutely! sō des ne!
accelerator akseru
accept uketorimas
accident jiko
  there's been an accident jiko des
accommodation heya
  we need accommodation for three san-nin
  no heya ga irimas
accurate seikaku (na)
ache: my back aches senaka ga itai des
across: across the road michi no mukō
  how do we get across? dō yat-te
  watarimaska?
adapter adaptā
address jūsho
  will you give me your address? jūsho o
  kudasaimas-ka?
adhesive bandage *(small)* bansōkō
adjust awasemas
admission *(charge)* nyūjōryō
advance: can we reserve in
  advance? maemot-te yoyaku dekimas-ka?
advertisement kōkoku
afraid: I'm afraid I don't know zan-nen-nagara
  shirimasen

I'm afraid so zan-nen-nagara sō des
I'm afraid not zan-nen-nagara dame des
after: after you dōzo o-saki ni
  after 2 o'clock niji kara
  after the meal shokuji no ato
afternoon gogo
  in the afternoon gogoni
  good afternoon kon-nichi wa
  this afternoon kyō no gogo
aftershave aftāshēbu
again mata
age toshi
  under age miseinen
  it takes ages nagaku kakarimas
ago: a week ago is-shūkan mae
  it wasn't long ago son-na ni mae no koto ja
  arimasen
  how long ago was that? dono kurai mae
  deshta-ka?
agree: I agree sansei des
  raw fish doesn't agree with me sashimi wa
  karada ni aimasen
air kūki
  by air hikōki de
  with air-conditioning reibō tski no
airport kūkō
alarm (for fire, etc.) keihō
alarm clock mezamashi-dokei
alcohol arukōru
alive: is he still alive? kare wa mada ikite
  imas-ka?
all zembu
  all these people kono hito-tachi zembu
  that's all ijō des
  that's all wrong zembu machigai des
  all right kek-kō des
  thank you – not at all arigatō – dō
  itashimashte
allergic: I'm allergic to penicillin penishirin ni
  arerugī des
allowed: is it allowed? ī des-ka?

that's not allowed dame des
allow me sumimasen
almost hotondo
alone hitori
  did you come here alone? hitori de koko ni
  kimashta-ka?
  leave me alone kamawanaide kudasai
already sude ni
also ...mo
altogether: what does that make
  altogether? zembu de ikura des-ka?
always itsumo
a.m.: at 8 a.m. gozen hachiji ni
ambassador taishi
ambulance kyūkyūsha
  get an ambulance! kyūkyūsha o yonde
  kudasai!
» *TRAVEL TIP: to call an ambulance, dial 119 if*
  you have someone speaking Japanese with you;
  otherwise ask an English-speaking operator by
  dialing 0051
America Amerika
American *(man, woman)* Amerika-jin
  (adjective) Amerika no
among... ...no naka de
amp: 13 amp fuse jū-san ampe-a hyūzu
and *(with nouns)* to
angry okot-te
  I'm very angry about it sono koto de hontō
  ni okot-te imas
  please don't get angry okoranaide kudasai
animal dōbutso
ankle ashikubi
anniversary: it's our wedding
  anniversary watashi-tachi no kek-kon
  kinenbi des
annoy: he's annoying me watashi o
  komarasemas
  it's very annoying totemo komarimas
another: can we have another room? betsu no
  heya o kudasai

another beer, please bīru o mō ip-pai kudasai

answer: what was his answer? henji wa dō deshta-ka?

there was no answer henji ga arimasen deshta

antique kot-tōhin

any: have you got any bananas/butter? banana/batā ga arimas-ka?

I haven't got any zenzen arimasen

anybody dareka

can anybody help? dareka tasukete kuremas-ka?

I don't know anybody in Tokyo Tōkyō de dare mo shirimasen

anything nanika

I don't want anything nanimo hoshiku arimasen

is there anything else? hoka ni nanika arimas-ka?

apartment apāto

aperitif shokuzenshu

apology: please accept my apologies hontō ni sumimasen

» *TRAVEL TIP: it is regarded as too direct to ask for an apology; but apologies such as "sumimasen" are freely offered in most cases—apart from, for example, on crowded public transport where often nothing will be said if you bump into a stranger; see* **sorry**

appendicitis mōchō-en

appetite shokuyoku

I've lost my appetite shokuyoku ga arimasen

apple rin-go

apple juice rin-goshu

(carbonated) saidā

application form mōshikomi-yōshi

appointment: can I make an appointment? yakusoku ga dekimas-ka?

apricot anzu

April shi-gatsu

area *(neighborhood)* kinjo

(space) ōkisa

in the area kono atari ni
arm ude
around... ...no mawari ni
  is he around? kare ga imas-ka?
arrange: will you arrange it? sore o keikaku
  shimas-ka
  it's all arranged keikakuzumi des
arrest (verb) taiho shimas
  he's been arrested kare wa taiho saremashta
arrival tōchaku
arrive tskimas
  we only arrived yesterday kinō tsuita
  bakari des
art bijutsu
art gallery bijutsukan
arthritis kansetsu-en
artificial jinkō no
artist geijutsuka
as: as quickly as you can dekiru dake hayaku
  as much as you can dekiru dake takusan
  do as I do watashi ga suru yō ni
  as you like o-ski na yō ni
ashtray haizara
Asia Ajia
ask tanomimas
  could you ask him to...? kare ni...o suru
  yō ni tanonde kudasai
  that's not what I asked for sore wa tanonda
  no ja arimasen
asleep: he's still asleep mada nemut-te imas
asparagus asparagas
aspirin aspirin
assistant (helper) joshu
  (in shop) tenin
asthma zensoku
at: at the café kis-saten de
  at my hotel watashi no hoteru de
  at one o'clock ichiji ni
atmosphere (in bar, etc.) funiki
  (weather) tenki
attitude taido

attractive miryoku-teki
   I think you're very attractive miryoku-teki
   des ne
August hachi-gatsu
aunt *(own)* oba
   (someone else's) oba-san
Australia Ōsutoraria
Australian *(man, woman)* Ōsutoraria-jin
   (adjective) Ōsutoraria no
authorities tōkyoku
automatic *(car)* jidō no
autumn: in the autumn aki ni
away: is it far away from here? koko kara tōi
   des-ka?
   go away! at-chi e ikinasai!
awful osoroshī
axle shajiku
baby akachan
   we'd like a baby-sitter komori ga hoshī des
» *TRAVEL TIP: baby-sitting is virtually unknown in*
   Japan, since the mother almost always stays
   with the baby, but close relatives may baby-sit
   on occasion
back: I've got a bad back senaka ga warui des
   I'll be back soon sugu modorimas
   is he back? kare wa modorimashta-ka?
   come back! modorinasai!
   can I have my money back? o-kane o
   kaeshte kuremas-ka?
   I go back tomorrow ashta uchi e kaerimas
   at the back ushiro ni
backpack ryukku sak-ku
bacon bēkon
   bacon and eggs bēkon eg-gu
bad warui
   it's not bad māmā des
   too bad! zan-nen des ne!
bad: the milk/meat is bad miruku/niku ga
   kusat-te imas
bag kaban
   (suitcase) sūtsukēsu

baggage tenimotsu
bakery pan-ya
balcony barukonī
  a room with a balcony barukonī no aru heya
ball bōru.
ballpoint pen bōru-pen
bamboo take
banana banana
band *(music)* bando
bandage hōtai
  could you change the bandage? hōtai o
  kaete kuremas-ka?
  small adhesive bandage bansōkō
bank ginkō
» *TRAVEL TIP: banks are open from 9 a.m. to*
3 p.m., closed on Saturdays and Sundays
bar bā
  when does the bar open? bā wa itsu
  akimas-ka?
» *TRAVEL TIP: no strict opening hours for bars, but*
lunchtime drinking is unusual; main activity
starts after dark and continues until 11 p.m.;
beware of bars that don't display a price list;
likewise politely refuse peanuts, snacks, etc.
unless you know how much you will have to
pay for extras; best to go to bars with a
Japanese acquaintance
barbershop toko-ya
bargain: it's a real bargain o-kaidoku des
barmaid josei no bāten
bartender bāten
baseball yakyū
basket kago
bath o-furo
  can I have a bath? o-furo ni hait-te mo ı des-ka?
  could you give me a bath towel? taoru o
  kudasai
» *TRAVEL TIP: remember that in Japan the bath is*
a place for relaxation after you've washed your-
self; if your host should offer you a bath, this is
an invitation to relax; don't get the water soapy!

bathing nyūyoku
bathing suit kaisuigi
bathrobe gaun
bathroom furoba
  **we want a room with a private
  bathroom** basutski no heya ga hoshī des
  can I use your bathroom? toire o tskat-te
  mo ī des-ka?
  where's the bathroom? o-tearai wa doko
  des-ka?
» *TRAVEL TIP: see* **toilet**
battery denchi
bay: Tokyo Bay Tōkyō wan
beach hama
beans mame
beautiful kirei (na)
  that was a beautiful meal oishī shokuji
  deshta
because... ...dakara
  because of... ...no tame ni
  because of the weather tenkō no tame ni
bed *(Western-style)* bed-do
  (Japanese-style) toko
  single bed/double bed shin-guru
  bed-do/daburu bed-do
  I want to go to bed nemuritai des
» *TRAVEL TIP: in Japanese-style accommodations a
  thick quilt, called a "futon," will be laid out on
  the tatami mats in your room; for a cover you
  will have a "kake-buton," the thickness of
  which will vary according to the season; your
  pillow or "makura" will feel harder than
  Western-style pillows*
bed and breakfast chōshoku-tski yado
bedroom shinshitsu
bee mitsubachi
beef gyūniku
beer bīru
  two beers, please bīru nihon onegai shimas
» *TRAVEL TIP: the usual type is lager, but other
  imported kinds are freely available at a price*

before: before breakfast chōshoku mae ni
   before we leave tatsu mae ni
   I haven't been here before koko ni kita koto
   ga arimasen
begin: when does it begin? itsu
   hajimarimas-ka?
beginner shoshinsha
behind... ...no ushiro ni
   the car behind me ushiro no kuruma
believe: I don't believe you shinji-raremasen
   I believe you anata o shinjimas
bell *(in hotel)* beru
belong: that belongs to me watashi no des
   whom does this belong to? kore wa dare no
   des-ka?
below shta ni
belt beruto
bend *(noun: in road)* kābu
berth *(on ship, train)* shindai
beside... ...no soba ni
best ichiban ī
   it's the best vacation I've ever had ima
   made de ichiban ī kyūka des
better mot-to ī
   have you got anything better? mot-to ī
   mono ga arimas-ka?
   are you feeling better? kibun ga yoku
   narimashta-ka?
   I'm feeling a lot better kibun ga zut-to yoku
   narimashta
between... ...no aida ni
beyond... ...no mukō ni
bicycle jitensha
big ōkī
   a big one ōkī no
   that's too big ōkisugimas
   it's not big enough jūbun ōkiku arimasen
   have you got a bigger one? mot-to ōkī no ga
   arimas-ka?
bikini bikini
bill o-kanjō

could I have the bill, please? o-kanjō o kudasai

» *TRAVEL TIP: restaurant bills, etc. are usually paid discreetly by the person who made the original invitation; going Dutch is common only among good friends; to reciprocate, make a return invitation*

bird tori

birthday tanjōbi

happy birthday! o-tanjōbi omedetō!

it's my birthday watashi no tanjōbi des

bit: just a little bit for me hon-no skoshi dake

that's a bit too expensive skoshi taka-sugimas

a bit of that cake sono kēki o skoshi

bite: I've been bitten *(by dog)* (inu ni) kamaremashta

(by insect) (mushi ni) sasaremashta

bitter *(taste)* nagai

black kuroi

she's had a blackout kizetsu shimashta

bland *(food)* aji no nai

blanket mōfu

I'd like another blanket mō ichimai mōfu ga hoshī des

bleed chi ga demas

his nose is bleeding hanaji ga dete imas

bless you!

» *TRAVEL TIP: sneezing evokes no comment in Japan, but using a handkerchief can cause embarrassment; use it very discreetly, by turning away from other people, for example*

blind *(cannot see)* mekura (no)

(on window) buraindo

blinding: his lights were blinding me raito de me ga kuramimashta

blind spot mōten

blister: I've got a blister on my finger yubi ni mame ga dekimashta

blonde *(noun)* brondo

blood ketsu-eki

his blood type is... kare no ketsu-eki-gata
wa...
I've got high blood pressure kō-ketsuatsu
des
he needs a blood transfusion yuketsu ga
irimas
Bloody Mary buradi-mēri
blouse brausu
blue aoi
board: full board sanshoku-tski
half board nishoku-tski
boarding pass tōjōken
boat fune
(small) bōto
when is the next boat to...? tsugi
no...yuki no fune wa itsu des-ka?
body karada
(corpse) shitai
boil *(noun)* haremono
do we have to boil the water? mizu o
wakasa-nakereba narimasen-ka?
boiled egg yude tamago
boiled rice gohan
bone hone
book *(noun)* hon
bookstore hon-ya
» *TRAVEL TIP: major bookstore chains also
stocking Western books in large cities are
Maruzen (Tokyo—near Tokyo Station) and
Kinukuniya (near Shinjuku Station in Tokyo)*
boot būtsu
border *(of country)* kok-kyō
bored: I'm bored taikutsu des
boring taikutsu (na)
born: I was born in... ...de umaremashta
see **date**
borrow: can I borrow...? ...o kashte
kuremas-ka?
boss bosu
both ryōhō
I'll take both of them ryōhō hoshī des

....

bottle bin
bottle opener sen-nuki
bottom: at the bottom of the hill oka no
fumoto ni
bouncer yōjimbō
bow o-jigi
» *TRAVEL TIP: while Japanese will bow to each
other on meeting, they might offer to shake your
hand since you are a foreigner; for your own
part a not-too-firm handshake together with a
slight bow will be in order*
bowels chō
bowl *(noun)* chawan
box hako
boy otoko no ko
boyfriend bōi-frendo
bra brajā
bracelet ude-wa
brakes burēki
  could you check the brakes? burēki o
  shirabete kudasai
  I had to brake suddenly kyū ni burēki o
  kake-nakereba narimasen deshta
  he didn't brake burēki o kakemasen
  deshta
brandy burandē
bread pan
  could we have some bread and butter?
  batā-tski pan o kudasai
  some more bread, please mot-to pan o
  kudasai
break *(verb)* kowashimas
  I think I've broken my arm ude o ot-ta to
  omoimas
breakable koware-yasui
breakdown: I've had a breakdown kuruma no
enko des
» *TRAVEL TIP: free help offered to foreign motorists
by Japan Automobile Federation (JAF)*
  nervous breakdown shinkei-suijaku
breakfast chōshoku

» *TRAVEL TIP: in most kinds of accommodations,
    except for the traditional inn (ryokan), you will
    have the choice of Western or Japanese-style
    breakfasts; Japanese-style is rice with a raw
    egg stirred in, soy bean soup, seaweed, and
    pickles*

breast chibusa
breath iki
  he's getting very short of breath iki ga
  kirete imas
breathe iki o shimas
  I can't breathe iki ga dekimasen
bridge hashi
briefcase shoruikaban
brilliant *(person, idea, swimmer)* subarashi
bring mot-te kimas
  could you bring it to my hotel? watashi no
  hoteru ni mot-te kite kudasai
Britain Eikoku
British Eikoku no
brochure pamfret-to
  **have you got any brochures
  about . . . ?** . . . no pamfret-to ga arimas-ka?
broken kowareta
  I've broken it kowashimashta
  it's broken kowarete imas
  my room/car has been broken into
  heya/kuruma ga arasare-mashta
brooch brōchi
brother *(own) (older)* ani
  (younger) otōto
  (someone else's) (older) o-nī-san
  (younger) o-tōto-san
brown cha-iroi
brown paper cha-iro no kami
browse: can I just browse around? mite
  mawat-te mo ī des-ka?
bruise *(noun)* uchimi
brunette *(noun)* brunet-to
brush *(noun)* brashi
bucket baketsu

Buddhism buk-kyō
buffet byuf-fe
building biru
bullet train shinkan-sen
bump: he bumped his head atama ni kobu ga
    dekimashta
bumper bampā
bunk shindai
bunk beds nidan bed-do
burglar dorobō
burned: this meat is burned kono niku wa
    kogete imas
    my arms are burned *(sunburned)* ude ga
    hiyake shimas
    **can you give me something for these
    burns?** yakedo o naosu kusuri o kudasai
bus bas
    tour bus chokyori-basu
    bus stop bastei
    bus tour kashkiri-basu no dantai
    **could you tell me when we get
    there?** tsuitara oshi-ete kudasai
» *TRAVEL TIP: long-distance bus travel in Japan is
    much slower than by rail, but it is cheaper; in
    the towns, buses tend to have destinations
    displayed in Japanese writing only*
business: I'm here on business shigoto de
    kimashta
business card meishi
» *TRAVEL TIP: obligatory to carry these if you're on
    business, a thoughtful gesture if you're a
    tourist; the Japanese attach great importance to
    the business card; if a Japanese gives you his
    card, study it carefully and place it at your side
    for reference during conversation*
business hotel bijines hoteru
» *TRAVEL TIP: cheaper and more basic; it's likely
    that English will not be spoken*
businessman bijinesman
business trip shutchō
businesswoman bijines ūman

bust basto
> *TRAVEL TIP: bust sizes*

US	32	34	36	38	40
Japan	80	87	91	97	107

busy *(streets, etc.)* isogashī
  the line's busy denwachū
  are you busy? isogashī des-ka?
but keredomo
  not this one but that one kore ja nakute, are
butcher shop niku-ya
butter batā
button botan
buy: I'll buy it kaimas
  where can I buy . . . ? doko de . . . o
  kaemas-ka?
by: I'm here by myself hitorikiri des
  are you by yourself? o-hitori des-ka?
  can you do it by tomorrow? ashta made ni
  dekimas-ka?
  by train/by car/by plane densha de/kuruma
  de/hikōki de
  who's it made by? dare ga tskurimashta-ka?
bye-bye bai-bai
cabaret kyabarē
cabbage kyabets
cabin *(on ship)* senshits
cable *(electric)* kēburu
café kis-saten
> *TRAVEL TIP: cafés or coffee shops are popular*
  places to meet in Japan; although the price of
  coffee may seem on the high side, Japanese
  cafés provide useful places to meet, particularly
  since the Japanese are hesitant to invite
  strangers to their homes; and for the price of
  just one cup of coffee you can relax or talk or
  listen to music for hours on end, without being
  obliged to order more
cake kēki
  a piece of cake kēki hitokire
calculator keisanki
call *(verb)* yobimas

....

will you call the manager? manejā o yonde kudasai
what is this called? kore wa nan to īmas-ka?
I'll call you (on the phone) denwa shimas
calligraphy shodō
calm (person, sea) shizuka (na)
calm down! ochitski nasai!
camera kamera
can[1]: kan
a can of beer kan-iri bīru
can-opener kankiri
can[2]: can I have...? ...o kudasai
can you show me...? ...o misete kudasai
I can't... koto ga dekimasen
he can't... kare wa...koto ga dekimasen
we can't... watashi-tachi wa...koto ga dekimasen
Canada Kanada
Canadian (person) Kanada-jin
cancel: I want to cancel my reservation yoyaku o torikeshtai des
can we cancel dinner for tonight? komban no yūshoku o torikeshte mo ī des-ka?
candle rōsoku
candy amai mono
cane sampo-yō no stek-ki
car kuruma
by car kuruma de
carafe mizusashi
carbonated tansan (no)
carburetor kyaburetā
card (name card) meishi
cards toramp
do you play cards? toramp o shimas-ka?
care: good-bye, take care sayonara, ki o tskete
will you take care of this suitcase for me? kono sūtsukēsu o mite ite kudasai
careful: be careful ki o tskete
car ferry kā-ferī
carp koi
carpet kāpet-to

carrot ninjin
carry: will you carry this for me? kore o
  mot-te kuremas-ka?
carving chōkoku
case *(suitcase)* sūtsukēsu
cash genkin
  I haven't any cash genkin wa zenzen
  arimasen
  will you cash a check for me? kogit-te o
  genkin ni shte kudasai
cash register kaikei
cassette kaset-to
cassette recorder kaset-to rekōdā
cat neko
catch: where do we catch the bus? doko de
  basu ni norimas-ka?
  he's caught a bug byōki ni narimashta
cathedral daiseidō
Catholic *(adjective)* Katorik-ku (no)
cauliflower karifurawā
cave hora-ana
ceiling tenjō
celery serori
cellophane serofan
center chūshin
  how do we get to the city center? machi no
  chūshin niwa dō ikimas-ka?
centigrade ses-shi
» *TRAVEL TIP: to convert C to F:* $\frac{C}{5} \times 9 + 32 = F$

  Centigrade −5 0 10 15 21 30 36.9
  Fahrenheit 23 32 50 59 70 86 98.4
centimeter senchi
» *TRAVEL TIP: 1 cm = 0.39 inches*
central chūshin (no)
central heating sentoraru hītin-gu
certain tashka (na)
  are you certain? tashka des-ka?
certificate shōmeisho
chain kusari
chair isu
champagne shampen

change: could you change this into yen? kore o en ni kaete kudasai
I don't have any change komakai o-kane ga arimasen
do we have to change trains? densha o norikae-nakereba narimasen-ka?
I'll just get changed chot-to kigaemas
character *(written)* kanji
charge: what will you charge? ikura des-ka?
who's the person in charge? sekininsha wa dare des-ka?
chart chāto
cheap yasui
have you got something cheaper? mot-to yasui no ga arimas-ka?
cheat: I've been cheated damasare-mashta
check¹: will you check? shirabete kudasai
I've checked shirabemashta
will you check the total? gōkei o shirabete kudasai
check² kogit-te
will you take a check? kogit-te de haraemas-ka?
» TRAVEL TIP: *checks are rarely used for daily transactions, cash or (sometimes) credit cards being preferred*
checkbook kogit-te-chō
cheek hoho
cheers *(toast)* kampai
cheese chīzu
say cheese! warat-te!
chef shef
chest mune
» TRAVEL TIP: *chest measurements*

US	36	38	40	42	44	46
Japan	90	95	100	105	110	115

chewing gum chūin-gam
chickenpox mizubōsō
child kodomo
children kodomotachi

children's portion o-kosama ranchi

» *TRAVEL TIP: restaurants on the top floor of large department stores cater to parents with young children*

chin ago

China Chūgoku

china setomono

Chinese *(adjective)* Chūgoku (no)

chocolate chokorēto

   hot chocolate kokoa

   a box of chocolates hakoiri chokorēto

choke *(car)* chōku

chop *(noun)* atsugiri

   pork/lamp chops atsugiri no pōku/ram

chopsticks hashi

» *TRAVEL TIP: when you've finished with your chopsticks, put them on the chopstick rest or lay them flat across your bowl; don't stick them upright in the rice; if taking food from a central dish, use the other end of the chopsticks from the one you've been putting in your mouth*

Christmas kurismas

» *TRAVEL TIP: although Japan is a non-Christian country, Christmas is nevertheless promoted by big business as a commercial event, especially with sales of ice cream cake, but Christmas presents are not (yet) exchanged; the big festival is New Year's*

chrysanthemum kiku

church kyōkai

   where is the Protestant/Catholic Church? Protestanto/Katorik-ku no kyōkai wa doko des-ka?

» *TRAVEL TIP: for times of church services, consult the English language newspapers published in Japan; only a few services are conducted in English though*

cigar hamaki

cigarette tabako

would you like a cigarette? tabako wa ikaga des-ka?

filtered or plain? firutā tski des-ka, firutā nashi des-ka?

circle maru

city toshi

claim *(insurance)* baishō yōkyū

clarify akiraka ni shimas

clean *(adjective)* kirei (na)

can I have some clean sheets? kirei na shītsu o kudasai

my room hasn't been cleaned today kyō, heya no sōji ga mada des

it's not clean kirei ja arimasen

clear: I'm not clear about it sore wa yoku wakarimasen

do you think it'll clear up later? ato de hareru to omoimas-ka?

clever kashkoi

climate kikō

» *TRAVEL TIP: in central Japan, spring is cold and wet and is followed by a hot and extremely rainy period between the middle of June and mid-July; the hot, muggy summer lasts till the beginning of September; during this time there can be typhoons (with a lot of rain); the dry autumn can last well into December; winter in the major city belt between Tokyo and Osaka is generally crisp, cold, and sunny; the north of Japan has cooler summers and more snow in winter; the south is muggier in summer with relatively mild winters*

clock tokei

clogs geta

close¹ *(nearby)* chikai

close²: when do you close? itsu shimemas-ka?

closed *(window)* shimat-te

(shop) heiten

cloth nunoji

(rag) zōkin

clothes yōfku

clothespin sentaku-basami
cloud kumo
club kurab
clutch krat-chi
  the clutch is slipping krat-chi ga suberimas
coast kaigan
coat *(overcoat, etc.)* kōto
coatroom kurōku-rūm
cockroach gokiburi
coffee kōhī
  coffee, please kōhī o kudasai
» *TRAVEL TIP: coffee, whether bought in tins or*
  drunk in coffee shops, is relatively expensive in
  Japan; the usual drink is green tea (o-cha),
  drunk without milk or sugar
coin kōka
cold *(adjective)* samui
  (water) tsumetai
  I'm cold samui des
  I've got a cold kaze o hīte imas
collapse: he's collapsed taoremashta
collar eri
» *TRAVEL TIP: collar sizes*

US	14	14.5	15	15.5	16	16.5	17
Japan	36	37	38	39	40	41	42

collect: I want to collect... ...o mot-te kitai
des
color iro
  have you any other colors? betsu no iro ga
arimas-ka?
comb kushi
come kimas
  I come from America Amerika shush-shin
des
  we came here yesterday kinō koko ni
kimashta
  come on! hayaku!
  come here koko ni kite kudasai
comfortable yut-tari shte imas
  it's not very comfortable chot-to yut-tari
shte imasen

comic book man-ga
Common Market Ōshū shijō
company *(business)* kaisha
  you're good company yoi nakama des ne
compartment *(train)* kyakushitsu
compass rashimban
compensation son-gai-baishō
complain kujō o īmas
  I want to complain about my room/the
  waiter heya/ueitā ni tsuite kujō o ītai des
completely kanzen ni
complicated: it's very complicated hijō ni
  fukuzatsu des
compliment: my compliments to the chef shef
  ni yoroshku
concert konsāto
concussion nōshintō
condition jōtai
  it's not in very good condition jōtai wa
  amari yoku arimasen
condom kondōm
conference kaigi
confession jihaku
confirm: I want to confirm . . . . . . o
  tashkametai des
confuse: you're confusing me watashi o
  konran sasemas
congratulations! omedetō!
conjunctivitis ketsumaku-en
con man pombiki
connection *(travel)* renraku
connoisseur tsū
conscious: he is conscious ishki ga arimas
consciousness: he's lost consciousness ishki
  ga nakushimashta
constipation bempi
consul ryōji
consulate ryōjikan
contact: how can I contact . . . ? . . . ni dō
  renraku dekimas-ka?
contact lens(es) kontakto-renz

contraceptive hinin
convenient benri (na)
cook: the cook kok-ku-san
   it's not cooked ryōri shte arimasen
   it's beautifully cooked totemo kirei ni ryōri
   shte arimas
cookie bisket-to
cool suzushī
corkscrew sen-nuki
corn *(foot)* uo no me
corner *(of street)* kado
   (table, room, box, etc.) sumi
   can we have a corner table? sumi no tēburu
   o onegai shimas
cornflakes kōn-frēku
correct tadashī
cosmetics keshōhin
cost: what does it cost? ikura des-ka?
   that's too much taka-sugimas
   I'll take it kudasai
» *TRAVEL TIP: bargaining is very unusual in
   Japan*
cough *(noun)* seki
cough syrup sekidome no shirop-pu
could: could you please...? ...o onegai
   shimas
   could I have...? ...o kuremas-ka?
country kuni
   in the country inaka ni
couple: a couple of... *(two)* ...futatsu *(a few)*
   ni-san no...
courier gaido
course: of course mochiron
court: I'll take you to court saibanzata ni
   shimas
» *TRAVEL TIP: the number of lawyers in Japan is
   very low as compared with the West; most
   disputes are settled out of court with the help of
   a go-between*
cousin itoko
cover: keep him covered up tsutsunde kudasai

cover charge sābisuryō
cow ushi
crab kani
crane *(bird)* tsuru
crash: there's been a crash shōtotsu des
crazy kichigai
  you're crazy! kichigai des!
  (milder statement) kawat-temas ne!
cream *(on milk, in cake, for face)* kurīm
crêche takujisho
credit card kurejit-to kādo
» *TRAVEL TIP: only of use in big department stores,*
  hotels, and restaurants—but they are becoming
  more widespread
crisis kiki
crossroads jūjiro
crowded konda
cruise junkō ryokō
crutch *(for invalid)* matsubazue
cry: don't cry nakanaide kudasai
culture bunka
cup *(china)* kap-pu
  (plastic, etc.) kop-pu
  a cup of Western-style tea kōcha ip-pai
cupboard todana
curry karē
curtains kāten
cushion *(Western)* kush-shon
  (Japanese) zabuton
Customs zeikan
cut: I've cut my hand te o kirimashta
cycle: can we cycle there? soko e jitensha de
  ikemas-ka?
cyclist saikuristo
cylinder shirindā
dad(dy) *(own)* chichi
  (someone else's) o-tō-san
damage: I'll pay for the damage benshō
  shimas
damaged kowareta
damn! ima-imashī !

damp shimet-ta
dance dansu
  would you like to dance? dansu o
  shimashō-ka?
dangerous abunai
dark kurai
  when does it get dark? itsu goro kuraku
  narimas-ka?
  dark blue kon
darling anata
dashboard keikiban
date: what's the date? nan-nichi des-ka?
  can we have a date? *(romantic)* dēto o
  shimashō-ka?
  can we fix a date? *(business)* itsu ga ī
  des-ka?
  on the fifth of May go-gatsu itsuka ni
  in 1951 sen kyūhyaku gojū ichinen ni
date *(fruit)* natsume-yashi no mi
daughter *(own)* musume
  (someone else's) musume-san
day hi
  have a good day yoi ichinichi o
dead shinda
deaf mimi ga tōi
deal: it's a deal sore de kimari des
  will you deal with it? sore o yat-te
  kuremas-ka?
dear
  Dear Sir/Madam haikei
  Dear Mr. Suzuki haikei
December jūni-gatsu
deck dek-ki
deck chair dek-ki-che-a
declare: I have nothing to declare shinkoku
  suru mono wa arimasen
deep fukai
  is it deep? fukai des-ka?
delay: the flight was delayed hikōki ga
  okuremashta
deliberately waza to

delicate *(person)* sensai (na)
delicious oishī
  it's delicious oishī des
  that was delicious go-chisōsama deshta
delivery: is there another mail delivery?
  yūbin no haitatsu ga mō ik-kai arimas-ka?
deluxe gōka (na)
democratic minshuteki (na)
dent *(noun)* hekomi
  you've dented my car kuruma o hekomase-
  mashta
dentist ha-isha
  YOU MAY HEAR...
  ōkiku akete kudasai *open wide please*
  amari itaku arimasen yo *this won't hurt much*
  itai des-ka? *does it hurt?*
  susuide kudasai *rinse out please*
dentures ireba
deny: I deny it hitei shimas
deodorant deodoranto
departure shup-patsu
depend: it depends on ... ... ni yorimas
deport tsuihō shimas
deposit atamakin
  do I have to leave a deposit? atamakin o
  haraimas-ka?
depressed yū-utsu (na)
depth fukasa
desparate: I'm desparate for a drink hidoku
  nodo ga kawakimas
dessert dezāto
destination mokutekichi
detergent senzai
detour: we have to make a detour via ...
  ... o tōt-te mawarimichi o shimas
devalued yasuku nat-ta
develop: could you develop these? kore o
  genzō shte kudasai
diabetic tōnyōbyō-kanja
dialing code shigai-kyokuban
diamond daiyamondo

diaper omutsu
diarrhea geri
  have you got something for diarrhea?
  geridome no kusuri ga arimas-ka?
diary *(personal)* nik-ki
  (business) techō
dictionary jisho
didn't *see* **not**
die shinimas
  he's dying shinimas
diesel *(fuel)* dīzero oiru
diet daiet-to
  I'm on a diet daiet-to-chū des
different: they are different chigaimas
  can I have a different room? chigau heya o
  onegai shimas?
  is there a different route? chigau rūto ga
  arimas-ka?
difficult muzukashī
digestion shōka
dining room shokudō
dinner yūshoku
  (midday) chūshoku
dinner jacket dinā jaket-to
direct *(adjective)* choksetsu (no)
  does it go direct? chok-kō shimas-ka?
dirty kitanai
disabled *(person)* shintai shōgaisha
disappear nakunarimas
  it's just disappeared nakunat-te
  shimaimashta
disappointing gak-kari
disco disko
  see you in the disco disko de aimashō
discount waribiki
disgusting iya (na)
dish *(food)* ryōri
  (plate) o-sara
dishonest fushōjiki (na)
disinfectant shōdokuzai
distance kyori

distress signal sōnan shin-gō
distributor *(car)* haidenki
disturb: the noise is disturbing us oto ga
 urusai des
divorced rikonshta
do: how do you do? hajimemashte, dōzo yoroshku
 what are you doing tonight? kon-ya nani o
 shimas-ka?
 how do you do it? dō yat-te shimas-ka?
 will you do it for me? shte kuremas-ka?
 I've never done it before mae ni shta koto
 ga arimasen
 I was doing 60 (kph) rokuju kiro de unten
 shte imashta
doctor isha
 (as form of address) sensei
 I need a doctor isha o onegai shimas
» *TRAVEL TIP: English-speaking doctors advertise
 in the small ads section of the English-
 language daily papers in Japan; if you need
 urgent help, phone the English-speaking
 information service (Tokyo 502-1461; from
 outside Tokyo: phone 104 and ask for Collect
 Call, T.I.C.—Tokyo Information Center); this
 service is only available during office hours
 however*
 YOU MAY HEAR…
 mae ni mo arimashta-ka? *have you had this
 before?*
 doko ga itai des-ka? *where does it hurt?*
 ima, don-na kusuri o nonde imas-ka? *what
 medicine/drugs are you taking at the moment?*
 ichi/ni jō nonde kudasai *take one/two*
 ichinichi ni ni/san kai *two/three times a day*
document shorui
dog inu
Dolls' Festival hinamatsuri
don't! dame! *see* **not**
door doa
 (in Japanese house to divide rooms) fusuma
 (to divide room from corridor) shōji

doorway genkan
dosage tōyaku-ryō
double room daburu
down: down the road michi o orite
   get down! orinasai!
downstairs kaika e
dress *(woman's)* dores
dressing *(for wound)* hōtai
   (for salad) doresh-shing-gu
drink *(noun)* nomimono
   (verb) nomimas
   would you like a drink? nomimono wa ikaga
   des-ka?
   I don't drink arukōru wa nomimasen
   I had too much to drink last night kinō
   nomi-sugimashta
   is the water drinkable? mizu wa
   nomemas-ka?
» *TRAVEL TIP: alcoholic drinks are freely available
--from vending machines as well; but drinking
should really only start after dark and usually
stops by 11 p.m.; "sake," the Japanese national
drink, is the general word for alcohol (as well
as meaning "rice wine")*
drive: I've been driving all day ichinichi-jū
   unten shimashta
» *TRAVEL TIP: the Japanese drive on the left*
driver unten-shu
driving license untem-menkyoshō
drown: he's drowning oborete imas
drug *(medical)* ksuri
   (narcotic) mayaku
drugstore kusuri-ya
drunk *(adjective)* yop-parat-ta
» *TRAVEL TIP: drunkenness among males is not
frowned upon as long as it occurs after dark
and in the right places, e.g., bars; this is
regarded as an excellent safety valve, but it is
not acceptable for women to show signs of
drunkenness*
dry kawaita

dry cleaner dorai-kurīning-gu-ya
due: when is the bus due? basu wa itsu
  kimaska?
during... ...no aida ni
dust hokori
duty-free *(adjective)* menzei
  (shop) menzeiten
dwarf trees bonsai
dynamo dainamo
each: can we have one of each? hitotsu zutsu
  kudasai
  how much are they each? hitotsu ikura
  des-ka?
ear mimi
  I have an earache mimi ga itai des
early hayai
  we want to leave a day earlier ichinichi
  hayaku detai des
earring iyaring-gu
earthquake jishin
east higashi
Easter fuk-kats-sai
easy yasashī
eat tabemas
  something to eat nanika taberumono
eel unagi
egg tamago
eggplant nasu
either: either...or... ...ka...ka
  I don't like either dochira mo ski ja arimasen
elastic gomuhimo
elbow hiji
electric denki (no)
electric heater denki hītā
electrical outlet konsento
electrician denkiya-san
electricity denki
» *TRAVEL TIP: voltage is 100; electric plugs are
  identical to those used in the United States—
  two flat pins*
electronic denshi

electronics erekutoroniksu
elegant jōhin (na)
elevator erebētā
  the elevator isn't working erebētā wa koshō
  des
else: something else nanika hoka no mono
  somewhere else dokoka hoka no tokoro
  who else? hoka ni dare-ka?
  or else sono hoka
embarrassed: I'm/she's embarrassed haji o
  kakimas
embarrassing hazukashī
embassy taishkan
emergency hijō
Emperor Ten-nō Heika
empty kara (no)
end owari
  when does it end? itsu owarimas-ka?
engaged *(person)* kon-yaku shta
engagement ring kon-yaku yubiwa
engine enjin
engine trouble enjin no koshō
England Igirisu
  English *(language)* Eigo
  I'm/he's American Amerikan-jin des
enjoy: I enjoyed it very much totemo
  tanoshkat-ta des
enlargement hikinobashi
enormous totemo ōkī
enough: thank you, that's enough arigatō,
  sore de jūbun des
entertainment goraku
entrance iriguchi
  (to house) genkan
envelope fūtō
equipment setsubi
  photographic equipment shashin yōgu
error machigai
escalator eskarētā
especially toku ni
essential hitsuyō (na)

it is essential that... ... koto ga hitsuyō des
Europe Yōrop-pa
even: even the Americans Amerika-jin demo
evening yūgata
  this evening komban
  good evening komban wa
evening dress *(for man)* yakaifuku
  (for woman) ibuning-gu dores
ever: have you ever been to...? ... e it-ta
  koto ga arimas-ka?
every subete no
  every day mainichi
everyone min-na
everything subete
everywhere doko demo
evidence shōko
exact tadashī
example rei
  for example tatoeba
excellent subarashī
except... ... igai
  except me watashi igai
excess chōka
excess baggage chōka tenimotsu
exchange *(verb: money)* ryōgae shimas
exciting omoshiroi
excursion ensoku
excuse me *(to get past, etc.)* shitsurei shimas
  (to get attention) chot-to sumimasen
  (apology) sumimasen
exhaust *(car)* haikikan
exhausted gut-tari shta
exit deguchi
expect: she's expecting ninshinchū des
expenses: it's on an expense account hitsuyō
  keihi des
expensive takai
  that's too expensive taka-sugimas
expert senmonka
explain setsumei shimas

would you explain that slowly? yuk-kuri
setsumei shte kudasai
export *(noun)* yushutsu
extra yobun no
  an extra glass/day yobun no guras/hi
  is that extra? sore wa tsuika des-ka?
extremely totemo
eye me
eyebrow mayu
eye shadow aishadō
eyewitness mokugekisha
face kao
face mask masku
» *TRAVEL TIP: to attempt to stop the spreading of*
  colds, face masks were introduced after the
  1918 flu epidemic; these cover nose and mouth
  and can be bought at pharmacies
fact jijitsu
factory kōjō
Fahrenheit kashi
» *TRAVEL TIP: to convert F to C:* $F - 32 \times \frac{5}{9} = C$

Fahrenheit	23	32	50	59	70	86	98.4
Centigrade	−5	0	10	15	21	30	36.9

faint: she's fainted kizetsu des
fair *(fun fair)* yūenchi
  (commercial) tenjikai
  that's not fair fukōhei des
faithfully: yours faithfully keigu
fake nise (no)
fall: he's fallen korobmashta
false machigat-ta
family kazoku
family altar butsudan
fan *(cooling)* sempūki
  (hand-held) (folding) sensu
  (non-folding) uchiwa
fan belt famberuto
far tōi
  is it far? tōi des-ka?
  how far is it? dono kurai tōi des-ka?

fare *(travel)* ryōkin
farm nōjō
farther mot-to tōku
fashion ryūkō
fast hayai
   don't speak so fast amari hayaku
   hanasanaide kudasai
fat *(adjective)* futot-ta
   (noun) abura
fatal(ly) chimeiteki (ni)
father *(own)* chichi
   (someone else's) o-tō-san
faucet jaguchi
fault ara
   it's not my fault watashi no sei ja arimasen
faulty chōshi ga okashī
favorite *(adjective)* ichiban ski (na)
fax faksu
February ni-gatsu
fed up: I'm fed up *(bored)* unzari shimashta
feel: I feel cold/hot samui/atsui des
   I feel like ... ... shtai des
ferry ferī
festival matsuri
fever netsu
   he's got a fever netsu ga arimas
few: only a few skoshi dake
   a few ... ni-san no ...
   a few days ni-san-nichi
fiancé(e) kon-yakusha
field nohara
fifty-fifty gobu-gobu
figs ichijiku
figure *(number)* sūji
   (of person) sugata
   I'm watching my figure futoranai yō ni
   shimas
fill: fill her up mantan ni shte kudasai
   to fill in a form yōshi ni kakikomimas
fillet hireniku

film *(cinema)* eiga
  (for camera) firum
  do you have this type of film? kon-na firum
  ga arimas-ka?
filter: filter or non-filter? firutā tski des-ka,
  firutā nashi des-ka?
find mitsukemas
  if you find it moshi mitsuketara
  I've found a ... ... o mitsukemashta
fine *(weather)* hareta
  a 10,000 yen fine sen-en no bak-kin
  OK, that's fine hai, ī des
finger yubi
fingernail tsume
finish owari
  I haven't finished owat-te imasen
fire: fire! kaji!
fire department shōbōtai
» *TRAVEL TIP: dial 119, and say "kaji des"*
fire extinguisher shōkaki
fireworks hanabi
first saisho (no)
  I was first ichiban deshta
first aid ōkyū teate
first aid kit kyūkyūbako
first class *(travel, etc.)* fāsto kuras
» *TRAVEL TIP: first class on trains is called
  "gurīn-sha" (green car)*
first name namae
» *TRAVEL TIP: more properly called "given" names,
  these are hardly ever used in Japan except
  towards younger members within a family and
  between very good friends who have known
  each other since childhood; as an outsider,
  therefore, avoid using first names unless
  specifically invited to do so; even then first
  name plus "-san" is better*
fish sakana
fix: can you fix it? naosemas-ka?
flag hata

....

flash *(photography)* frash-shu
flat *(adjective)* taira (na)
   this drink is flat ki ga nukete imas
   I've got a flat (tire) taiya ga panku
   shimashta
flavor aji
flea nomi
flight hiko
flippers furip-pa
flirt *(verb)* ichatskimas
float *(verb)* ukimas
floor yuka
   on the second floor ni-kai ni
   which floor? nan-kai des-ka?
flower hana
   bunch of flowers hanataba
flower arranging ikebana
flu ryūkan
fly *(insect)* hae
   (trousers) chak-ku
foggy kasunda
follow tsuite ikimas
food tabemono
food poisoning shoku-chūdoku
foot ashi
» *TRAVEL TIP: 1 foot = 30.5 cm = 0.3 meters*
for... ...no tame ni
   this is for you kore wa anata (no tame) ni des
   that's for me watashi no des
   that's for her kanojo no des
forbidden kinjirareta
foreign gaikoku (no)
foreigner gaikoku-jin
foreign exchange gaikoku-kawase
forget: I forget, I've forgotten wasuremas,
   wasurete shimai-mashta
   don't forget wasurenaide kudasai
   I'll never forget you anata o kesh-shte
   wasuremasen
fork fōku
form *(document)* yōshi

formal keishkiteki (na)
fortnight ni-shūkan
forward: could you forward my mail? yūbin o
okut-te kuremas-ka?
forwarding address iten saki
fracture kos-setsu
fragile koware-yasui
France Furansu
fraud sagi
free *(no cost)* tada (no)
(no work, etc.) hima (na)
freight kamotsu
french fries furench-frai
freshen up: I want to freshen up o-mekashi o
shtai des
Friday kin-yōbi
fried egg medama-yaki
friend tomodachi
friendly shtashī
from: from England/London Igirisu/Rondon
kara
where is it from? doko kara des-ka?
front *(noun)* mae
in front of you anata no mae ni
in the front mae ni
frost shimo
frozen ko-ot-ta
fruit kudamono
fry agemas
nothing fried agemono wa dame des
frying pan furai pan
fuel nenryō
Fuji: Mount Fuji Fuji-san
full ip-pai
fun: it's fun tanoshī des
funny *(strange)* okashī
(comical) omoshiroi
furniture kagu
further mot-to tōku
fuse fyūzu
fuss ōsawagi

future shōrai
  in the future kore kara
gale ōkaze
gallon garan
» *TRAVEL TIP: 1 gallon = 3.78 liters*
gallstones tanseki
galoshes nagagutsu
gamble gamburu shimas
garage *(repair)* shūrikōjō
garbage gomi
  (parking) shako
garden niwa
garlic nin-niku
gas gas
gasket gasket-to
gasoline gasorin
gas pedal akseru
gas station gasorin stando
» *TRAVEL TIP: only one grade of gasoline is sold,*
  and there is no self-service
gay *(homosexual)* homo (no)
gear *(car)* giya
  (equipment) dōgu
  I can't get it into gear giya ga hikemasen
gear lever giya rebā
geisha (girl) geisha
general delivery kyokudome
Germany Doitsu
gesture miburi
» *TRAVEL TIP: Japanese gestures are, on the whole,*
  less expansive than Western ones; some gestures
  that can be misunderstood are making a circle
  with index finger and thumb means "ok" in the
  West but "money" in Japan; a thumbs-up
  gesture means "ok" in the West but "boss" or
  "boyfriend" in Japan
get: will you get me a...? ...o motte kite
  kudasai
  will you come and get me? mukae ni kite
  kuremas-ka?

how do I get to . . . ? e dō ikeba ī des-ka?
when can I get it back? itsu kaeshte
moraemas-ka?
when do we get back? itsu modorimas-ka?
where do I get off? doko de orimas-ka?
where do I get a bus for . . . ? doko
de . . . yuki no basu ni noremas-ka?
have you got . . . ? . . . ga arimas-ka?
gin jin
  gin and tonic jin-tonik-ku
girl on-na no ko
  my girlfriend watashi no gāru-frendo
give *(I give to someone)* agemas
  (someone gives to me) kuremas
  will you give me . . . ? . . . o kuremas-ka?
  I gave it to him sore o agemashta
glad ureshī
glass garasu
  (drinking) kop-pu
  a glass of water o-mizu ip-pai
glasses *(eye)* megane
glue nori
go ikimas
  I want to go to Osaka Ōsaka ni ikitai des
  when does the bus go? itsu basu wa
demas-ka?
  it's/he's gone demashta
  I want to go *(leave)* sorosoro ikimas
  my car won't go kuruma ga ugokimasen
goal *(sport)* gōru
goat yagi
go-between nakōdo
God kami
goddess megami
gold kin
golf gorufu
good ī
  good! ī des!
good-bye sayonara
  (informal) de-wa mata

» *TRAVEL TIP: if someone has invited you for a meal then, on leaving, instead of saying "good-bye" you can say: go-chisōsama deshta—which means literally "it was a feast"*

gooseberries marusuguri

gram guram

» *TRAVEL TIP: 100 grams = approx. 3.5 oz.*

grand *(wonderful)* subarashī

grandfather *(own)* sofu
  (someone else's) o-ji-san

grandmother *(own)* sobo
  (someone else's) o-bā-san

grandson/granddaughter *(own)* mago
  (someone else's) o-mago-san

grapefruit gurēp-furūts

grapefruit juice gurēp-furūts jūsu

grapes budō

grass kusa

grateful kansha (no)
  I'm very grateful to you totemo kansha shimas

gratitude kansha

gravy gurēbī

gray hai-iro (no)

grease abura
  (for machinery) gurīsu

greasy abura-poi

great *(large)* ōkī
  (major) sugoi
  great! sugoi!

greedy yokubari (no)

green midori-iro (no)

green car *(railway)* gurīn-sha

greengrocer yao-ya

green tea o-cha

grocery shokuryōhin-ten

ground *(soil)* tsuchi
  (area) guraundo
  on the ground jimen ni
  on the ground floor ik-kai ni

group gurūpu

our group leader gurūpu rīdā
I'm with the American group Amerika-jin
no grūpu des
guarantee hoshō
  is there a guarantee? hoshō ga arimas-ka?
guest o-kyaku
» *TRAVEL TIP: if you are invited to a Japanese
home it will be a great honor, since most
entertaining is done in restaurants; take a
nicely wrapped present, ideally something from
home; see also* **manners**
guest house minshuku
» *TRAVEL TIP: for details on private guest houses,
which are less expensive than hotels or Japanese-
style inns, you can contact the Nihon Minshuku
Center in Tokyo*
guide gaido
guilty yūzai (no)
guitar gitā
gum *(in mouth)* haguki
  (for chewing) chūin-gam
gun *(pistol)* pistoru
gynecologist fujinka no o-isha-san
hair kami
hairbrush burashi
haircut sampatsu
  (for women) kat-to
hairdresser's *(for men)* toko-ya
  (for women) bi-yō-in
half hambun
  a half portion hambun
  half an hour sanjup-pun
ham ham
hamburger hambāgā
hammer kanazuchi
hand te
handbag handobag-gu
handbrake handoburēki
handkerchief hankachi
handle *(noun)* handoru
hand luggage tenimotsu

....

handmade tezukuri (no)
handsome hansam (na)
hanger han-gā
hangover futska-yoi
  my head is killing me atama ga totemo itai des
happen: I don't know how it happened dōshte sō nat-ta ka wakarimasen
  what's happening/happened? nan des-ka/deshta-ka?
happy ureshī
harbor minato
hard katai
  (difficult) muzukashī
hard-boiled egg kata-yude tamago
harm *(noun)* gai
hat bōshi
hate: I hate... ...ga kirai des
have mochimas
  can I have...? ...o kudasai
  can I have some water/some more? o-mizu/mot-to kudasai
  I have no... ...ga arimasen
  do you have any cigars/a map? hamaki/chizu ga arimas-ka?
  I have to leave tomorrow asu denakereba narimasen
hayfever kafunshō
he kare
  he is American Amerika-jin des
  he has left demashta
head atama
headache zutsū
headlights hed-do raito
head waiter kyūjichō
health kenkō
  your health! kampai!
healthy kenkō (na)
hear: I can't hear kikoemasen
hearing aid hochōki
heart shinzō

heart attack shinzō mahi
heat atsusa
heater *(electric)* denki hītā
heating dambō
heat stroke nish-shabyō
heavy omoi
heel *(of foot)* kakato
   (of shoe) hīru
   could you put new heels on these? atarashī
hīru o tskete kudasai
height takasa
hello chot-to
   (on telephone) moshi-moshi
helmet herumet-to
help *(noun)* taske
   can you help me? taskete kudasai
   help! taskete!
her kanojo
   I like her kanojo ga ski des
   with her kanojo to
   to her kanojo ni
   her... kanojo no...
   it's her bag, it's hers kanojo no bag-gu des,
kanojo no des
here koko
   come here koko ni kite kudasai
high takai
highway kōsoku-dōro
hill oka
him kare
   I don't know him kare o shirimasen
   with him kare to
   to him kare ni
hire karimas
his kare no
   it's his drink, it's his kare no nomimono des,
kare no des
hit: he hit me nagurare-mashta
hitchhike hit-chi haiku shimas
hold *(verb)* mochimas
hole ana

holiday *(national)* shuku-saijitsu
» *TRAVEL TIP: public holidays are 1st January,
2nd–4th January (National Bank Holidays),
15th January (Coming-of-Age Day or Adults'
Day), 11th February (National Foundation
Day), 21st March approx. (Vernal Equinox
Day), 29th April (Green Day–formerly
Emperor Hirohito's birthday), 3rd May
(Constitution Memorial Day), 5th May
(Children's Day), 15th September (Respect for
the Aged Day), 23rd September approx.
(Autumnal Equinox Day), 10th October (Health
and Sports Day), 3rd November (National
Culture Day), 23rd November (Labor
Thanksgiving Day), 23rd December (Emperor
Akihito's birthday)*
home *(own)* uchi
  (someone else's) o-taku
  I want to go home kaeritai des
  at home uchi ni/o-taku ni
homesick: I'm homesick hōmu-shik-ku ni
narimashta
honest shōjiki (na)
  honestly? hontō ni?
honey hachimitsu
honeymoon shinkon ryokō
hood *(car)* bon-net-to
hope *(noun)* kibō
  I hope that ... ... suru to ī des ne
  I hope so sō da to ī des ne
  I hope not sō ja nai to ī des ne
horn *(car)* keiteki
horrible osoroshī
hors d'oeuvre ōdōburu
horse uma
hospital byōin
» *TRAVEL TIP: hospitals with some English-
speaking staff in Japan's two largest cities are
St. Luke's Hospital, Tokyo, (03) 541-5151, and
Yodogawa Hospital, Osaka, (06) 322-2250*
host shujin-yaku

....

hostess *(in the house)* shufu-yaku
  (in a bar, cabaret, etc.) hostes
hot atsui
  (spiced) karai
hotel *(Western-style)* hoteru
  (Japanese-style) ryokan
hour jikan
house *(building)* ie
  see also **home**
housewife shufu
how dō
  how many? ikutsu des-ka?
  how much? *(price)* ikura des-ka?
  how often? nankai kurai?
  how often do the trains go? *(per day)*
  ichijikan ni nambon des-ka?
  (per hour) ichinichi ni nambon des-ka?
  how long does it take? dono kurai
  kakarimas-ka?
  how long have you been here? dono kurai
  koko ni imas-ka?
  how are you? o-genki des-ka?
  YOU MAY THEN HEAR...
  okagesama de, genki des *I'm fine, thank you
  very much*
  māma des *so-so*
humid mushiatsui
humor yūmo-a
  haven't you got a sense of humor? yūmo-a
  no sensu ga arimas-ka?
» *TRAVEL TIP: humorous remarks should be made
  with caution; social satire is rare due to fear of
  "loss of face"; beware of making jokes about
  Japan or the Japanese, even if, in your view,
  the jokes are quite harmless*
hungry: I'm hungry onaka ga suite imas
  I'm not hungry onaka ga suite imasen
hurry: I'm in a hurry isoide imas
  please hurry! isoide kudasai!
hurt: it hurts itamimas
  my leg hurts ashi ga itamimas

husband *(own)* shu-jin
    (someone else's) go-shu-jin
I watashi
    I am American/I am a teacher Amerika-jin
    des/sensei des
ice kōri
    with lots of ice taksan no kōri to
ice cream ais-kurīm
iced coffee ais-kōhī
identity papers mimoto shōmeisho
idiot baka
» *TRAVEL TIP: this is one of the strongest*
swearwords used in public: be very careful
when you feel like using it; if in doubt, say
nothing or try to smile, since the whole idea of
swearing is considered uncivilized
if moshi
ignition *(car)* tenkasōchi
ill byōki (no)
    I feel ill kibun ga warui des
illegal hōritsu ihan (no)
illegible yominikui
illness byōki
immediately sugu
import *(noun)* yu-nyū
important taisetsu (na)
    it's very important totemo taisetsu des
import duty yu-nyūzei
impossible fukanō (na)
impressive inshōteki (na)
improve kaizen shimas
    I want to improve my . . . watashi no . . . o
    kaizen shtai des
in: in America/Tokyo Amerika/Tōkyō ni
    in English Eigo de
inch inchi
» *TRAVEL TIP: 1 inch = 2.54 cm*
include fukumemas
    does that include breakfast? chōshoku tski
    des-ka?

inclusive fukumete
incompetent yaku ni tatanai
inconsiderate omoiyari no nai
incredible shinjirarenai
indecent migurushī
independent dokuritsu (no)
India Indo
Indian *(noun)* Indo-jin
indicator injikētā
indigestion shōka-furyō
indoors okunai de
industry san-gyō
infection densen
infectious densensei (no)
inflation infre
informal hikōshiki (no)
information jōhō
　　do you have any information in English
　　on...? ...ni tsuite Eigo de jōhō ga
　　arimas-ka?
　　is there an information office? an-naijo ga
　　arimas-ka?
inhabitant *(house)* jūnin
　　(city) jūmin
injection chūsha
injured kega o shta
　　he's been injured kega o shimashta
injury kega
innocent tsumi no nai
insect mushi
insect repellent mushiyoke
inside *(adverb)* naka ni
insist: I insist shuchō shimas
insomnia fuminshō
instant coffee instanto kōhī
instead: instead of... ...no kawari ni
　　can I have that one instead? kawari ni are o
　　kudasai
insulating tape zetsuen-tēpu
insulation zetsuen

insult bujoku
» TRAVEL TIP: *unintentional insults could be touching a Japanese, ignoring seniority, talking too loudly, making jokes about Japan and the Japanese*
insurance hoken
intelligent atama no ī
interesting omoshiroi
international koksaiteki (na)
interpreter tsūyakusha
　　would you interpret for us? tsūyaku o onegai shimas
into... ...ni
introduce: can I introduce...? ...o shōkai shimas
　　(formal) ...o go-shōkai mōshiagemas
invalid *(noun)* byōnin
invitation shōtai
　　thank you for the invitation go-shōtai o arigatō gozaimas
invite: can I invite you out? go-shōtai shte ī des-ka?
Ireland Airurando
Irish: I'm Irish Airurando-jin des
iron *(noun: for clothes)* airon
　　will you iron these for me? airon o kakete kudasai
island shima
it sore
　　it is... sore wa...des
Italy Itaria
itch *(noun)* kayusa
　　it itches kayui des
itemize: would you itemize it for me? meisai o onegai shimas
» TRAVEL TIP: *it is not very polite to ask for itemized bills in Japanese restaurants, especially if you are entertaining, since it shows a lack of trust in the management*
jack *(car repair)* jak-ki
jacket jaket-to

jam jam
   traffic jam kōtsū mahi
January ichi-gatsu
Japan Nihon
Japanese *(adjective)* Nihon (no)
   (language) Nihon-go
   (person, people) Nihon-jin
   in Japanese Nihon-go de
Japanese bedding futon
Japanese chess shōgi
Japanese flute shakuhachi
Japanese food Nihon ryōri
Japanese harp koto
Japanese inn ryokan
Japanese-style wafū
Japanese tea o-cha
jaw ago
jealous yakimochi (no)
jeans jīnz
jellyfish kurage
jewelery hōseki
job shigoto
joke *(noun)* jōdan
   you must be joking! jōdan deshō!
journey ryokō
judo jūdō
July shichi-gatsu
junction *(of roads)* kōsaten
June roku-gatsu
junk *(rubbish)* gomi
just: just two *(only)* futatsu dake
   just there *(right)* sugu soko
   not just now ima sugu ja naku
   just now *(a little while ago)* chot-to mae ni
   that's just right chōdo ī des
keep: can I keep it? morat-te ī des-ka?
   you keep it sono mama de ī des
   you didn't keep your promise yakusoku o
mamorimasen deshta
   keep the change otsuri wa kek-kō des
» *TRAVEL TIP: tipping is not necessary in Japan*

ketchup kechap-pu
kettle yakan
key kagi
kidney jinzō
kill *(verb)* koroshimas
kilo kiro

» *TRAVEL TIP: conversion:* $\frac{kilos}{5} \times 11 = pounds$

kilos	1	1.5	5	6	7	8	9
pounds	2.2	3.3	11	13.2	15.4	17.6	19.8

kilometer kiromētoru

» *TRAVEL TIP: conversion:* $\frac{kilometers}{8} \times 11 = miles$

kilometers	1	5	10	20	50	100
miles	0.62	3.11	6.2	12.4	31	62

kind: that's very kind of you go-shinsetsu ni
dōmo
   what kind of...? dono yō na...?
kiss *(noun)* kis
kitchen daidokoro
knee hiza
knife naifu
knock *(verb)* nok-ku shimas
know shirimas
   I don't know shirimasen
Korea Kankoku
Korean *(adjective)* Kankoku (no)
label *(noun)* raberu
laces *(shoe)* kutsu no himo
lacquer shik-ki
ladies *(toilet)* fujin-yō toire
lady fujin
lake mizuumi
lamb *(meat)* ram-niku
lamp rampu
lamppost gaitō
lampshade rampu no kasa
land *(noun)* riku
lane *(car)* shasen
language kotoba
large ōkī
laryngitis kōtōen

last saigo (no)
  last year kyonen
  last week senshū
  last night yūbe
  at last! tōtō!
late: sorry I'm late okurete sumimasen
  it's a bit late skoshi osoi des
  please hurry, I'm late isoide kudasai,
  okurete imas
  at the latest osokutomo
later ato de
  see you later mata ato de
laugh *(verb)* waraimas
laundrette koinrandorī
laundry detergent senzai
law hōritsu
lawyer ben-goshi
laxative gezai
lazy namakemono
leaf ha
leak *(noun)* moreguchi
  it leaks moremas
learn: I want/she wants to learn ... ... o
  naraitai des
lease *(verb)* chin-gashi shimas
least: at least skunaktomo
leather kawa
leave: we're leaving tomorrow ashta demas
  when does the bus leave? bas wa itsu
  demas-ka?
  I left two shirts in my room heya ni shatsu
  o nimai nokoshimashta
  can I leave this here? koko ni kore o oite
  okemas-ka?
left hidari
  on the left hidari ni
left-handed hidarikiki (no)
left luggage (office) azukarisho
leg ashi
legal hōritsujō (no)
lemon remon

lemonade remonēdo
lend: will you lend me your . . . ? . . . o kashte kudasai
lengthen nagaku shimas
lens renz
less mot-to skunaku
  less than that sore ika, sore yori skunaku
let: let me help tetsudai-mashō-ka?
  let me go! hanashte kudasai!
  will you let me off here? koko de oroshte kudasai
  let's go ikimashō
letter tegami
  are there any letters for me? watashi ni tegami ga arimas-ka?
lettuce retas
liable *(responsible)* sekinin no aru
library toshokan
license menkyo
license plate nambā purēto
lid futa
lie *(untruth)* uso
  can he lie down for a bit? skoshi yoko ni naremas-ka?
life seikatsu
lifeboat kyūmei bōto
life insurance seimei hoken
lift *(noun)*: **do you want a lift?** norimas-ka?
  could you give me a lift? nosete kuremas-ka?
light[1]: **the lights aren't working** denki ga tsukimasen
  have you got a light? hi ga arimas-ka?
  when it gets light akaruku nat-tara
light[2] *(not heavy)* karui
light bulb denkyū
  the light bulb's gone out denkyū ga kiremashta
light meter roshutsukei
like: would you like . . . ? . . . ga hoshī des-ka?
  I'd like a . . . . . . ga hoshī des
  I'd like to . . . . . . o shtai des

I like it/you sore/anata ga ski des
I don't like it sore ga ski ja arimasen
what's it like? dō des-ka?
  do it like this kono yō ni shte kudasai
lime *(for drinks)* raim
line sen
line *(for tickets, etc.)* retsu
» *TRAVEL TIP: the concept of lining up is very
  similar to the American one; to let someone go
  ahead of you, say "o-saki no dōzo!"*
lip kuchibiru
lip salve rip-pu kurīm
lipstick kuchibeni
liqueur rikyūru
list *(noun)* risto
listen! kīte kudasai
liter rit-toru
little skoshi
  a little ice/a little more kōri/mō skoshi
  just a little skoshi dake
live sunde imas
  I live in America Amerika ni sunde imas
  where do you/does she live? doko ni sunde
  imas-ka?
liver *(medical)* kanzō
  (food) rebā
lizard tokage
loaf pan-ik-kin
lobster ise-ebi
local: could we try a local sake? jizake o
  tameshi-mashō-ka?
  a local restaurant jimoto no restoran
lock: the lock's broken kagi ga kowarete imas
  I've locked myself out kagi o heya ni oita
  mama, doa a shimete shimaimashta
lonely sabishī
long nagai
  we'd like to stay longer mot-to nagaku
  tomaritai des
  that was long ago mō zuibun mae no koto
  deshta

look: you look tired tsukarete imas ne
  I'm looking forward to ... ... o tanoshimi ni shte imas
  I'm looking for ... ... o sagashte imas
  I'm just looking mite iru dake des
  look out! ki o tskete!
loose *(handle, button, etc.)* yurui des
lose nakusimas
  I've lost my bag bag-gu o nakushimashta
  excuse me, I'm lost sumimasen, michi ni mayoimashta
lost property (office) otoshimono azukarisho
lot: a lot/lots taksan
  a lot of bread/sake taksan no pan/o-sake
  a lot more expensive hijō ni takai
lotion rōshon
loud *(noise)* urusai
  (voice) ōkī
  louder mot-to urusai/ōkī
love: I love you anata ga ski des
  do you love me? watashi ga ski des-ka?
  he's in love koi shte imas
  I love sake sake ga ski des
lovely utskushī
low hikui
luck un
  good luck! kō-un o!
lucky kō-un (na)
  you're lucky kō-un des ne
  that's lucky! yokat-ta des ne!
luggage nimotsu
lumbago yōtsū
lump *(in body)* kobu
lunch chūshoku
lung hai
luxurious zeitaku (na)
luxury zeitaku
mad kichigai (no)
made-to-measure ōdā mēdo (no)
magazine zash-shi
magnificent subarashī

maid *(Western-style hotel)* meido-san
   (Japanese-style inn) jochū-san
maiden name kyūsei
mail *(noun)* yūbin
   mailbox tegami-uke
main road ōdōri
make tskurimas
   will we make it in time? maniaimas-ka?
   made in Japan Nihonsei (no)
makeup keshō
man otoko no hito
manager manējā
   can I see the manager? manējā ni awasete
   kudasai
manicure manikyua
manners manā
» *TRAVEL TIP: proper behavior in Japan is very
important and takes a good deal of experience
to master as it is intimately related with the
correct use of language; however, Japanese tend
to make allowances for foreign visitors,
especially first-time visitors*
many taksan (no)
map chizu
   a map of . . . . . . no chizu
maple tree momiji
March san-gatsu
margarine māgarin
mark: there's a mark on it kizu ga arimas
market māket-to
marketplace ichiba
marmalade māmarēdo
married kek-kon shta
marry: will you marry me? kek-kon shte
   kuremas-ka?
martial arts budō
mascara maskara
massage mas-sāji
mat mat-to
   (thick, made from rice straw) tatami
   (thin, made from rice straw) goza

match mat-chi
  a box of matches mat-chi hitohako
material *(cloth)* kiji
matter: it doesn't matter dō demo ī des
  what's the matter? dō shtan des-ka?
mattress mat-tores
maximum saidai (no)
May go-gatsu
may: may I have...? ...o kudasai
maybe sō kamo shiremasen
mayonnaise mayonēzu
me watashi
  for me watashi no tame ni
  can you hear me? kikoemas-ka?
meal shokuji
mean: what does this mean? kore wa dō iu imi
des-ka?
measles hashka
  German measles fūshin
measurements sumpō
meat niku
mechanic: is there a mechanic here? koko ni
shūrikō ga imas-ka?
medicine kusuri
meet aimas
  when can we meet again? itsu mata
aemas-ka?
  pleased to meet you hajimemashte
» *TRAVEL TIP: after saying "hajimemashte" on
being introduced the correct continuation is:*
Harris des, dōzo yoroshku *I'm Mr. Harris, how
do you do?*
  YOU MAY THEN HEAR...
kochira koso, dōzo yoroshku *the pleasure's
mine, how do you do?*
meeting kaigi
melon meron
member membā
  how do I become a member? dō yat-te
membā ni naremas-ka?
men's *(toilet)* otoko no hito-tachi

mend: can you mend this? kore o naoshte
kudasai
mention: don't mention it dō itashimashte
menu menyū; *see pages 62–72*
  can I have a menu, please? menyū o
kudasai
mess yogore
message: are there any messages for me?
mes-sēji ga arimas-ka?
  can I leave a message for ...? ... ni
mes-sēji o onegai shimas?
meter mētoru
» *TRAVEL TIP: 1 meter = 39.37 inches = 1.09
yards*
midday shōgo
middle man-naka
  in the middle man-naka ni
midnight mayonaka
might: I might be late osoku naru kamo
shiremasen
  he might have gone it-te shimat-ta kamo
shiremasen
migraine hen-zutsū
mild *(taste)* maroyaka (na)
  (weather) odayaka (na)
  (person) yasashī
mile mairu
» *TRAVEL TIP: conversion:* $\frac{miles}{5} \times 8 = kilometers$

miles	0.5	1	3	5	10	50	100
kilometers	0.8	1.6	4.8	8	16	80	160

milk miruku
  a glass of milk miruku ip-pai
milkshake mirukusēki
millimeter mirimētoru
minced meat hikiniku
mind: I've changed my mind ki ga
kawarimashta
  I don't mind ī des yo
  do you mind if I...? ... shte mo ī des-ka?
  never mind daijōbu des yo
mine watashi no

Menu *(in Western-style restaurants)*
See also the rest of the *Travelmate* word list

ōdoburu	**hors d'oeuvres, appetizers**
ōdoburu moriawase	assorted appetizers
sarami	salami
sumōku samon	smoked salmon
sarada	salad
kaki	oysters
sūpu	**soups**
kōn sūpu	(sweet) corn soup
consome sūpu	clear soup
potāju sūpu	thick soup
tamago ryōri	**egg dishes**
omuretsu	omelette
gyokai-ryōri	**seafood**
ise-ebi	lobster
kaki	oysters
sake	salmon
shtabirame	sole
hotategai	scallops
niku ryōri	**meat dishes**
katsuretsu	escalope
sāroin	sirloin
stēki	steak
bifuteki	beef steak
hireniku	fillet
rōsto bīfu	roast beef
rōsto pōku	roast pork
hambāgā	hamburger
karē raisu	curry and rice
tori-ryōri	**poultry dishes**
ahiru	duck
uzura	quail
niwatori	chicken
shichimenchō	turkey

yasai	**vegetables**
kyūri	cucumbers
jagaimo	potatoes
furench-frai	french fries
ninjin	carrots
negi	leeks
pīman	pimiento, green peppers
retasu	lettuce
nasu	eggplant
kudamono	**fruit**
orenji	oranges
suika	watermelon
banana	banana
budō	grapes
mikan	tangerines
rin-go	apples
dezāto	**desserts**
ais-kurīm	ice cream
ap-puru-pai	apple pie
kēki	cake
sufure	soufflé
chokorēto sandē	chocolate sundae
nomimono	**drinks**
bīru	beer (lager)
sake	Japanese rice wine
wain	wine
burandē	brandy
jin tonik-ku	gin and tonic
onza-rok-ku	scotch on the rocks
shōchū	drink like whisky but lighter
sherī	sherry
koka kōra	Coca-Cola
kōhī	coffee
frūtsu jūs	fruit juice
miruku	milk
kōcha	tea (Western-style)
o-cha	tea (Japanese-style)
mineraru uōtā	mineral water
remōnedo	lemonade

....

Menu *(in Japanese-style restaurants)*

Food Categories

にほんりょうり・日本料理
Nihon ryōri　　　food prepared Japanese-style

ちゅうごくりょうり・中国料理
Chūkoku ryōri　　food prepared Chinese-style

せいようりょうり・西洋料理
seiyō ryōri　　　food prepared Western-style

かいせきりょうり・懐石料理
kaiseki ryōri　　Japanese haute cuisine

ていしょく・定食
teishoku　　　set meal of rice, soup, pickles and
　　　　　　main dish

べんとう・弁当
bentō　　　lunch box, usually containing rice,
　　　　　meat and vegetables

ろばたやき・炉端焼
robatā-yaki　　fish and vegetables charcoal-
　　　　　　grilled

すし・寿司/鮨
sushi　　　raw fish on balls of rice

てっぱんやき・鉄板焼
tep-pan-yaki　　beef and vegetables grilled at the
　　　　　　table

すきやき・すき焼き
sukiyaki　　beef and vegetables cooked in a
　　　　　pot at the table

てんぷら・天麩羅
tempura　　vegetables or seafood deep-fried

おこのみやき・お好み焼き
okonomi-yaki　　batter with meat, fish and/or
　　　　　　vegetables, fried like pancakes at
　　　　　　the table

おでん・お田
oden   mixed fish and vegetables boiled in fish broth

…どんぶり・…丼
. . . domburi   bowl of rice with something (e.g. eel, shrimp) on top

なべもの・鍋物
nabemono   meat, fish and vegetables cooked in a pot

かまめし・釜飯
kamameshi   rice casserole dishes at the table

Vegetables

サラダ
sarada   salad

のり
nori   paper-like seaweed (dried)

しゅんぎく・春菊
shungiku   chrysanthemum greens

あぶらあげ・油揚げ
abura-age   fried bean curd

たくあん
takuan   yellow radish pickles

うめぼし
umeboshi   pickled plums

まつたけ
matsutake   Japanese mushrooms

なっとう
nat-tō   fermented soybeans

みそ
miso   fermented soybean paste

かんぴょう
kampyō   dried gourd shavings

とうふ
tōfu   bean curd

Soups

コンソメスープ
konsome sūpu   consommé

すましじる・清汁
sumashijiru   clear soup with vegetables or fish

みそしる・味噌汁
misoshiru   soup with fermented soybean paste

コーンスープ
kōn sūpu   (sweet) corn soup

Egg dishes

ゆでたまご・茹卵
yude-tamago   boiled egg

めだまやき・目玉焼き
medama-yaki   fried egg

たまごやき・卵焼き
tamago-yaki   Japanese-style omelette

おやこどんぶり・親子丼
oyako-domburi   bowl of rice with chicken and onion cooked in egg on top

ちゃわんむし・茶碗蒸し
chawam-mushi   light egg custard served hot, as side dish with shrimp, etc.

Rice dishes

ごはん・御飯
gohan   rice, as eaten with Japanese dishes

ライス
rais   rice, as eaten with Western-style dishes (mostly as side dish)

ちゅうかどんぶり・中華丼
chūka domburi   bowl of rice with pork and vegetables, in the Chinese style

チャーハン
chāhan   fried rice

オムライス
omurais   rice with a plain omelette wrapped around it

もち・餅
mochi   rice cakes

おにぎり
onigiri   rice balls

おちゃづけ・お茶漬
ochazuke   rice immersed in tea or fish broth

カレーライス
karē rais   rice with a curry-flavored meat stew

Noodles and noodle dishes

ラーメン
rāmen   Chinese noodles

うどん
udon   thick white wheat-flour noodles

そうめん・素麺
sōmen   thin white wheatflour noodles

そば・蕎麦
soba   buckwheat noodles

ざるそば・笊蕎麦
zaru soba   noodles served cold, to be dipped in soy sauce

やきそば・焼そば
yaki soba   fried noodles with small pieces of vegetables

ギョーザ
gyōza   dumplings filled with minced pork

チャンポン
champon   Chinese noodles with vegetables in salted bouillon

たぬきうどん
tanuki udon   noodles in fish stock with small pieces of deep-fried flour

Fish and seafood

さしみ・刺し身
sashimi   thinly sliced raw fish

やきざかな・焼魚
yaki-zakana   broiled fish

あわび・鮑
awabi   abalone, a kind of shellfish

ふぐ
fugu   blowfish — can be poisonous, thus served only in specially licensed restaurants

かつお
katsuo   bonito (tunny)

こい
koi   carp

はまぐり
hamaguri   clams

たら
tara   cod

かに
kani   crab

うなぎ
unagi   eel

にしん nishin	herring
あじ aji	horse mackerel
くらげ kurage	jellyfish
たこ tako	octopus
かき kaki	oyster
とろ toro	pink belly of the tuna fish
さけ sake	salmon
いわし iwashi	sardines
たい tai	sea bream
なまこ namako	sea slug
うに uni	sea urchin
えび ebi	shrimp
いか ika	squid
まぐろ maguro	tuna fish
ぶり buri	yellow tail

Sushi dishes

ごもくずし・五目寿司 gomokuzushi	mixed 'sushi' (raw fish)

いなりずし
inarizushi   seasoned rice wrapped in fried bean curd

かっぱまき
kap-pamaki   seasoned rice and cucumber wrapped in seaweed

のりまき
norimaki   sliced rice roll, fish powder and vegetables wrapped in seaweed

にぎりずし
nigirizushi   raw fish on rice balls

Meat and meat dishes

ぎゅうにく・牛肉
gyūniku   beef

ぶたにく・豚肉
butaniku   pork

とりにく・鳥肉
toriniku   chicken (and other fowl)

ビフテキ
bifuteki   beef steak

とんかつ・豚カツ
tonkatsu   deep-fried pork cutlets

カツどん・カツ丼
katsudon   deep-fried pork on rice

やきにく・焼肉
yakiniku   fried pork marinated in soy sauce

くしやき・串焼
kushiyaki   meat grilled and served on skewers

ハンバーグステーキ
hambāgu stēki   hamburger steak

ロースト ビーフ
rōsto bīfu · · · · · · · roast beef

ソーセージ
sōsēji · · · · · · · sausage

しょうがやき・生姜焼
shōgayaki · · · · · · · meat cooked in soy sauce with ginger

やきとり・焼鳥
yakitori · · · · · · · skewered grilled pieces of chicken

しゃぶしゃぶ
shabushabu · · · · · · · cooking one's own food at the table—usually sliced beef and vegetables

Desserts

くだもの・果物
kudamono · · · · · · · fruit

フルーツサラダ
frūtsu sarada · · · · · · · fruit salad

みつまめ・蜜豆
mitsumame · · · · · · · gelatin cubes with unsweetened beans

ところてん・心太
tokoroten · · · · · · · strips of gelatin

あんみつ・餡蜜
am-mitsu · · · · · · · gelatin cubes with sweet beans

おかし・お菓子
o-kashi · · · · · · · general term for confectionery

おせんべい・お煎餅
o-sembei · · · · · · · rice crackers

まんじゅう・饅頭
manjū · · · · · · · rice-flour cakes with bean jam

ようかん・羊かん
yōkan · · · · · · · sweet, soft bean paste

Seasoning

からし・辛子
karashi　　　　　　mustard

わさび
wasabi　　　　　　horseradish (very sharp)

しょうゆ・醤油
shōyu　　　　　　soy sauce

あじのもと・味の素
ajinomoto　　　　　　multi-seasoning flavor enhancer

Drinks

ビール
bīru　　　　　　beer

こうちゃ・紅茶
kōcha　　　　　　black (Western-style) tea

コーヒー
kōhī　　　　　　coffee

コーラ
kōra　　　　　　cola

おちゃ・お茶
o-cha　　　　　　Japanese (green) tea

ミルク
miruku　　　　　　milk

ミネラルウォーター
mineraru uōtā　　　　mineral water

オレンジジュース
orenji jūs　　　　　　orange juice

さけ・酒
sake　　　　　　rice wine (sake)

みず・水
mizu　　　　　　water

ワイン
wain　　　　　　wine

mineral water mineraru uōtā
minimum saishō (no)
minus mainasu
minute fun
  in a minute sugu
  just a minute chot-to mat-te kudasai
mirror kagami
Miss: Miss Jones Jones-san
miss: I miss you anata ga inakte sabishī des
  he's missing yukue-fumē des
  there is a . . . missing . . . ga mitskarimasen
mist kiri
mistake machigai
  I think you've made a mistake machigaeta
  to omoimas yo
misunderstanding gokai
modern modan (na)
mom *(own)* haha
  (someone else's) o-kā-san
Monday getsu-yōbi
money o-kane
  I've lost my money o-kane o nakushimashta
  they've taken all my money dorobō ni o-kane
  o zembu toraremashta
month tski
  one month hito-tski
moon tski
moped tansha
more mot-to
  can I have some more? mot-to kudasai
  more beer, please mot-to bīru o kudasai
  no more, thanks mō irimasen
  more comfortable mot-to raku (na)
  more than . . . . . . yori mot-to
morning asa
  good morning ohayō gozaimas
  in the morning gozenchū ni
  this morning kesa
mosquito ka
mosquito net ka-ya

most: I like it the most ichiban ski des
  most of the time/the people hotondo no
  jikan/hito
motel mōteru
mother *(own)* haha
  (someone else's) o-kā-san
motor mōtā
motorbike ōtobai
motorboat mōtābōto
motorcyclist ōtobai no saikuristo
motorist doraibā
mountain yama
mouse nezumi
moustache kuchihige
mouth kuchi
mouth-watering totemo oishī
move: don't move ugokanaide kudasai
  could you move your car? kuruma o
  ugokashte kudasai
movie eiga
  movie theater eigakan
» *TRAVEL TIP: seats at the movies tend to be*
  relatively expensive; non-Japanese films are
  usually shown in their original language, with
  Japanese subtitles
Mr.: Mr. Hamilton Hamilton-san
Mrs.: Mrs. Cummings Cummings-san
Ms: Ms Campbell Campbell-san
much taksan (no)
  much better daibu yoi
  much more mot-to taksan
  not much amari taksan ja naku
muffler sairensā
mug: I've been mugged gōtō des
muscle kin-niku
museum hakubutskan
mushroom *(Japanese or Chinese)* shītake
  (Western) mash-shurūm
music on-gaku
must: I must ... ... shinakereba narimasen
  I must not eat ... ... o taberare-masen

you must... anata wa...shinakereba narimasen

must I...? shinakereba narimasen-ka?

mustard karashi

my watashi no

my hotel watashi no hoteru

nail *(finger)* tsume

(wood) kugi

nail clippers tsumekiri

nail file tsumeyō yasuri

nail polish manikyua

nail scissors tsumekiriyō hasami

naked hadaka (no)

name namae

first name senreimei

my name is... watashi no namae wa...des

what's your name? o-namae wa nan des-ka?

» *TRAVEL TIP: Japanese put their surnames in front of their first names when talking about themselves and others or use just the surname; to address a Japanese use surname plus "-san" for both sexes; always omit "-san" when talking about yourself, since "-san" is a sign of respect*

napkin napukin

narrow semai

national kuni (no)

nationality kokseki

natural shizen (no)

naughty: don't be naughty itazura shinaide kudasai

near: is it near? chikai des-ka?

near here koko no chikaku

do you go near...? ...no chikaku e ikimas-ka?

where's the nearest...? ichiban chikai...wa doko des-ka?

nearly hotondo

neat *(drink)* storēto (no)

necessary hitsuyō (na)

it's not necessary hitsuyō wa arimasen

neck kubi
necklace nek-kures
need: I need a... ...ga irimas
needle hari
neighbor kinjo no hito
neither: I want neither... nor...
   ...mo...mo irimasen
   neither do I watashi mo...-masen
nephew *(own)* oi
   (someone else's) oigo-san
nervous shinkeishtu (na)
net *(fishing)* ami
net price seika
never kesh-shte
new atarashī
   New Year o-shōgatsu
   New Year's Eve ōmisoka
   Happy New Year akemashte omedetō
   gozaimas
» *TRAVEL TIP: when you hear the bell ring 108*
   times just before midnight, exchange the above
   greeting; it can be used up until January 7th
   for anybody you haven't met since January 1st
news nyūsu
newspaper shimbun
   do you have any English newspapers? Eiji
   shimbun ga arimas-ka?
newsstand shimbun-ya
New Zealand Nyūjīrando
New Zealander Nyūjīrando-jin
next tsugi (no)
   please stop at the next corner tsugi no kado
   de tomat-te kudasai
   see you next year rainen aimashō!
   next week raishū
   next Tuesday tsugi no ka-yōbi
   sit next to me tonari ni suwat-te kudasai
nice yoi
   (food, drink) oishī
niece *(own)* mei
   (someone else's) meigo-san

night yoru
  good night o-yasumi-nasai
  at night yoru ni
nightclub naito-kurabu
  is there a good nightclub here? koko ni yoi
  naito-kurabu ga arimas-ka?
nightlife naito-raifu
night porter yoru no momban
no īe
  there's no water zenzen mizu ga arimasen
  I have no money zenzen o-kane ga arimasen
  no way! dame des!
» *TRAVEL TIP: "īe" is rarely used for "no," except to
  answer factual questions; it sounds too abrupt;
  Japanese usually phrase personal questions so
  that they can be answered in the affirmative*
nobody dare mo . . . -masen
  nobody saw it dare mo sore o mimasen deshta
noisy urusai
  our room is too noisy heya wa urusa-sugimas
none dare mo . . . -masen
  none of them *(persons)* dare no . . . -masen
  (things) dore mo . . . -masen
nonsense bakageta
normal seijō (na)
north kita
Northern Ireland Kita Airurando
nose hana
nosebleed hanaji
not -masen
  not that one sore ja arimasen
  not me/you watashi/anata ja arimasen
  not here/there koko/asoko ja arimasen
  I'm not hungry onaka ga suite imasen
  I don't want to . . . . . . shtaku arimasen
  he didn't tell me watashi ni īmasen deshta
» *TRAVEL TIP: avoid negative questions in Japan;
  to the question "didn't you go?" a Japanese
  tends to answer "yes" if he/she did not go
  (confirming what you said) and "no" if he/she
  did go*

nothing nani mo . . . -masen
  there's nothing left nani mo nokot-te imasen
  nothing for me, thanks irimasen dōmo
November jūichi-gatsu
now ima
nowhere doko ni mo . . . -masen
  there's nowhere to sit doko ni mo
  suwaremasen
nude nūdo
nuisance: it's a nuisance meiwaku des
  this man's being a nuisance kono hito wa
  meiwaku des
numb shibireta
number ban-gō
nurse kan-gofu
nut *(for eating)* nat-tsu
  (for bolt) nat-to
obligatory kyōseiteki (na)
obviously akiraka ni
occasionally tokidoki
occupied *(toilet)* shiyōchū
  is this seat occupied? dare ka imas-ka?
o'clock: 3 o'clock sanji *see also* **time**
October jū-gatsu
octopus tako
odd *(number)* kisū
  (strange) kawat-ta
odometer sōkōkyorikei
of no
  the name of the hotel hoteru no namae
off: it just came off sugu toremashta
  10% off jū-pāsento biki
offense *(legal)* hanzai
office jimusho
officer *(to policeman)* o-mawari-san
official *(noun)* kōmuin
often yoku
  not often met-ta ni
oil oiru
  will you change the oil? oiru o kōkan shte
  kudasai

ointment nankō
OK kek-kō
old *(person)* toshi o tot-ta
  (thing) furui
  how old are you? nansai des-ka?
  I am 25 nijūgosai des
omelette omuretsu
on... ...no ue ni
  on the bar bā no ue ni
  I haven't got it on me ima mot-te imasen
  on Friday kin-yōbi ni
  on television terebi de
once ichido
  at once sugu
one hitotsu
  the red one akai no
one-way: a one-way to... ...made no
  katamichi
onion tamanegi
only... ...dake
open *(door, shop, etc.)* aita
  (exhibition, market, etc.) hiraita
  I can't open it akeru koto ga dekimasen
  when do you open? itsu akemas-ka?
opera opera
operation shujutsu
  will I need an operation? shujutsu ga
  irimas-ka?
operator *(telephone)* kōkanshu
opposite: opposite the hotel hoteru no mukai
optician meganeya
or mata wa
orange *(fruit)* orenji
  (color) orenji-iro (no)
orange juice orenji jūsu
order: could we order now? ima chūmon
  dekimas-ka?
  thank you, we've already ordered dōmo, mō
  chūmon shimashta
  (noun: in commerce) chūmon
Oriental Tōyō (no)

....

other: the other one hoka no
  do you have any others? hoka no mo
  arimas-ka?
otherwise sō de nakereba
ought: I ought to go ikubeki des
ounce
» *TRAVEL TIP: 1 ounce = 28.35 grams*
our: our hotel watashi-tachi no hoteru
  that one's ours sore wa watashi-tachi no des
out: we're out of gas gasorin-gire des
  get out! denasai!
outdoors kogai de
outlet *(electrical)* konsento
outside: can we sit outside? soto ni
  suwarimashō-ka?
over: over here/there koko/asoko ni
  over ... *(more than)* ... ijō
  it's all over subete owari des
overboard: man overboard! hito ga
  ochimashta!
overcharge: you've overcharged me yokei ni
  tot-te imas yo
» *TRAVEL TIP: in Japanese it's better etiquette to be
  more indirect, e.g., by saying "is this bill
  correct?"–o-kanjō wa ta-te imas-ka?*
overcooked nisugi (no)
overexposed roshutsu kado (no)
overnight *(travel)* ip-paku
oversleep nebō shimas
  I overslept nebō shimashta
overtake oitsukimas
owe: what do I owe you? ikura des-ka?
own: my own ... watashi jishin no ...
  are you on your own? o-hitori des-ka?
  I'm on my own hitori des
owner mochinushi
oxygen sanso
oyster kaki
Pacific Taiheiyō
pack: I haven't packed yet mada nizukuri shte
  imasen

page *(of book)* pēji
  could you page him? yobi-dashte kudasai
pain itami
  I've got a pain in my chest mune ga
  itamimas
pain-killers itamidome
painting e
pajamas pajama
pale aojiroi
pancake hot-to-kēki
panties pantī
pants zubon
paper kami
  (newspaper) shimbun
paper folding origami
parcel kozutsumi
pardon? *(didn't understand)* nan des-ka?
  I beg your pardon *(sorry)* sumimasen
parents *(own)* ryōshin
  (someone else's) go-ryōshin
park *(noun)* kōen
  where can I park my car? doko ni kuruma o
  chūsha dekimas-ka?
parking lot chūshajō
part bubun
partner *(boyfriend, girlfriend)* tsure
  (business) kyōdō kei-eisha
party *(group)* dantai
  (celebration) pātī
  I'm with the . . . party . . . dantai des
pass *(mountain)* tōge
  he's passed out ishiki ga nakunari-mashta
passable *(road)* tōreru
passenger jōkyaku
passerby tsūkōnin
passport pasupōto
past: in the past mae ni
  see time
pastry *(cake)* kēki no kiji
path komichi
patient: be patient shimbō shte kudasai

pattern moyō
pay haraimas
  can I pay, please? o-kanjō o onegai shimas
» *TRAVEL TIP: in bars, etc., it is usual to pay on leaving, not when ordering; tips are not necessary*
peace *(calm, not war)* heiwa
peach momo
peanuts pīnat-tsu
pear *(Japanese)* nashi
  (Western) yōnashi
pearl shinju
peas gurīmpīs
pedal *(noun)* pedaru
pedestrian hokōsha
pedestrian crossing ōdanhodō
» *TRAVEL TIP: pedestrians should behave like other road-users—even on empty roads they should wait for the green light before crossing*
pelvis kotsuban
pen pen
  have you got a pen? pen ga arimas-ka?
pencil empitsu
penicillin penishirin
penknife kogatana
pen pal pemparu
pensioner nenkin juryō-sha
people hitobito
  the Japanese people Nihon no jinkō
  two people futari
pepper koshō
peppermint pepāminto
per: per night/per week/per person ip-paku/shū/hitori
percent pāsento
perfect kampeki (na)
  the perfect vacation totemo subarashī kyūjitsu
perfume kōsui
perhaps tabun

period *(of time)* jiki
  (menstruation) seiri
permanent *(hair)* pāma
permit *(noun)* kyoka
person hito
  in person chokusetsu
pharmacist yak-kyoko
pharmacy kusuri-ya
» *TRAVEL TIP: if you need imported brands try the*
  shopping arcades of international hotels or The
  American Pharmacy in downtown Tokyo;
  traditional, Chinese-derived medicines will
  also be on display in pharmacies
phone *see* **telephone**
phonecard terefon kādo
photograph shashin
  would you take a photograph of us?
  shashin o tot-te kudasai
piano piano
pickpocket suri
picture e
pie *(fruit)* pai
piece hitokire
  a piece of... ...hitokire
pig buta
pigeon hato
pill piru
  are you on the pill? piru o nonde imas-ka?
» *TRAVEL TIP: the Japanese medical establishment*
  regards the pill with suspicion; condoms are
  the preferred method of birth control
pillow makura
pin pin
pinball pachinko
pine matsu
pineapple painap-puru
pint
» *TRAVEL TIP: 1 pint = 0.47 liters*
pipe paipu
  (for water) suidōkan

pipe tobacco paipu tabako
pity: it's a pity zan-nen des
place basho
  is this place taken? dare ka imas-ka?
  do you know any good places to go? yoi
  basho o shit-te imas-ka?
plain *(not patterned)* muji (no)
  plain food kantan no tabemono
plane hikōki
  by plane hikōki de
plant *(noun)* shokubutsu
plastic puraschik-ku
plastic bag binīrū-bukuro
plastic wrap serofan
plate sara
platform *(station)* hōmu
  which platform, please? dono hōmu des-ka?
play *(verb)* asobimas
  (theater) shibai
pleasant kimochi no ī
please: could you please...? ...-te kudasai
  please do dōzo
  excuse me, please onegai shimas
  yes, please (hai) onegai shimas
pleasure tanoshimi
  it's a pleasure dō itashimashte
plenty: plenty of... taksan no...
  thank you, that's plenty dōmo, jūbun des
pliers penchi
plug *(electrical)* sashikomi
  (sink) haisuisen
» *TRAVEL TIP: see* **electricity**
plum *(tree)* ume no ki
  (Japanese fruit) ume
  (Western fruit) puram
plumber haikankō
plus purasu
p.m.: at 8 p.m. gogo hachiji ni
pneumonia hai-en
poached egg otoshi tamago
pocket poket-to

point: could you point to it? sashte kudasai
  four point six yon ten roku
points *(car)* pointo
police keisatsu
  get the police keisatsu o yonde kudasai
» *TRAVEL TIP: in emergencies, dial 110 for the*
  police; these calls need no coins at call boxes;
  sometimes there are special phones next to the
  ordinary phones with only the numbers 110
  and 119 (for fire)
policeman keikan
police station keisatsusho
polish *(noun)* tsuyadashi
  will you polish my shoes? kutsu o migaite
  kudasai
polite teinei (na)
politics seiji
polluted kitanai
pool *(swimming)* pūru
poor: I'm very poor taihen bimbō des
  poor quality otot-ta hinshitsu
popular popyurā (na)
population jinkō
pork butaniku
port *(harbor)* minato
  (drink) pōto wain
porter *(in hotel)* pōtā
  (at station, etc.) akabō
portrait shōzōga
posh *(hotel, etc.)* rip-pa na
possible kanō (na)
  could you possibly . . . ? . . . -te itadakemas-ka?
postcard hagaki
post office yūbin-kyoku
» *TRAVEL TIP: the sign for a post office is [T̄];*
  opening hours are 9 to 5 on weekdays and 9 to
  12:30 on the first and fourth Saturdays of the
  month; mailboxes are usually painted red
potato jaga-imo
  sweet potato satsuma-imo
  potato chips poteto-chip-pu

pottery tōki
pound *(weight)* pondo
» *TRAVEL TIP: conversion:* $\frac{pounds}{11} \times 5 = kilos$

pounds	1	3	5	6	7	8	9
kilos	0.45	1.4	2.3	2.7	3.2	3.6	4.1

pour: it's pouring doshaburi des
powder *(for face)* kona-oshiroi
power outage teiden
prawns kuruma-ebi
prefer: I prefer this one kore ga ski des
pregnant ninshin shte imas
prescription shohōsen
present: at present ima wa
  here's a present for you purezento des, dōzo
» *TRAVEL TIP: exchanging presents is an important
  part of Japanese etiquette; presents shouldn't be
  too cheap or too expensive; they should be
  properly wrapped (department stores will do
  this for you); it is impolite to open a present in
  front of the giver, although exceptions are often
  made in the case of Westerners*
president *(of country)* daitōryō
  (of firm) shachō
press: could you press these? airon o kakete
  kudasai
pretty kirei (na)
  pretty good kanari yoi
price nedan
priest *(Catholic)* bokshi
  (Buddhist) o-bō-san
printed matter insatsubutsu
prison keimusho
private praibēto
probably tabun
problem mondai
product seihin
profit ri-eki
promise: do you promise? yakusoku
  shimas-ka?
  I promise yakusoku shimas
pronounce hatsuon shimas

how do you pronounce this? dō hatsuon shimas-ka?
properly tadashiku
property mochimono
prostitute baishunfu
protect mamorimas
Protestant protestanto (no)
proud hokori o mot-ta
prove: I can prove it shōmei dekimas
public: the public kōshū
public bath sentō
pudding pudin
  (dessert) dezāto
pull *(verb)* hikimas
  he pulled out in front of me kyū ni watashi no mae ni demashta
pump pompu
punctual: he's very punctual taihen jikan o mamorimas
puncture panku
puppet nin-gyō
puppet theater bunraku
pure *(cotton, etc.)* junsui (na)
purple murasaki (no)
purse saifu
push *(verb)* oshimas
  don't push osanaide kudasai
put: where can I put...? ...o doko ni okimashō-ka?
quality hinshitsu
quarantine ken-eki kikan
quarter yombun no ichi
  a quarter of an hour jūgofun
quay hatoba
question shitsumon
quick hayai
quiet shizuka (na)
  be quiet! shizuka ni shte kudasai!
quite: quite a lot zuibun taksan
radiator hōnetsu-ki
  (in car) rajiētā

radio rajio
rail: by rail densha de
rain ame
  it's raining ame ga fut-te imas
raincoat reinkōto
rainy season tsuyu
rally *(car)* rarī
rape *(noun)* bōkō
rare mare (na)
  (steak) rea
raspberry ki-ichigo
rat dobu-nezumi
rather: I'd rather sit here mushiro koko ni
  suwarimas
  I'd rather not go mushiro ikimasen
  it's rather hot yaya atsui des
raw nama (no)
razor kamisori
razor blades kamisori no ha
read: you read it yonde kudasai
  something to read yomimono
ready: when will it be ready? itsu
  dekimas-ka?
  I'm not ready yet mada yōi ga dekimasen
real hontō (no)
really hontō ni
rearview mirror bak-ku mirā
reasonable mot-tomo (na)
receipt ryōshūsho
  can I have a receipt please? ryōshūsho o
  onegai shimas
recently saikin
reception *(at company)* uketske
  (desk at hotel) fronto
  (for guests) resepshon
  at the reception desk uketske de/fronte de
receptionist *(at company)* uketske-gakari
  (at hotel) fronto-gakari
» *TRAVEL TIP: if a Japanese asks to meet you "at*
  the front of the hotel" it may mean the
  "fronto"–the reception desk

recipe tskurikata
recommend: can you recommend...? ...o
  oshiete kudasai
record *(music)* rekōdo
red akai
reduction *(in price)* nesage
refrigerator kin-yōbi
refuse: I refuse kotowarimas
region chihō
registered letter kakitome
regret: I have no regrets kōkai wa arimasen
relax: I just want to relax chot-to yasumitai
  des
  relax! raku ni shte kudasai!
religion shūkyō
remember: don't you remember? obo-ete
  imasen-ka?
  I'll always remember... itsumo...o
  omoidashimas
  something to remember you by omoide
  toshte
rent: can I rent a car/bicycle? kuruma/jitensha
  o kashte kudasai
repair: can you repair it? naosemas-ka?
repeat: could you repeat that? mō ichido
  onegai shimas?
reputation hyōban
rescue *(verb)* kyūjo shimas
reservation yoyaku
  I want to make a reservation yoyaku shtai
  des
reserve: can I reserve a seat? seki o yoyaku
  dekimas-ka?
responsible sekinin no aru
rest: I've come here for a rest kyūyō no tame
  ni koko ni kimashta
restaurant restoran
rest room *see* **toilet**
retired taishoku shta
reverse gear bak-ku gia
rheumatism ryūmachi

rib abarabone
rice *(uncooked)* o-kome
   (cooked, with Japanese food) go-han
   (cooked, with Western food) rais
rice bowl chawan
rich *(person)* kanemochi (no)
   (food) shitskoi
ridiculous bakageta
right: that's right sō des
   you're right sono tōri des
   on the right migite ni
   right now ima sugu
   right here masa ni koko
right-hand drive migi handoru (no)
  » *TRAVEL TIP: Japanese cars have right-hand
    drive since the Japanese drive on the left*
ring *(on finger)* yubiwa
ripe juku shta
rip-off: it's a rip-off taka-sugimas ne!
river kawa
road michi
   which is the road to...? ...yuki no michi
  wa dore des-ka?
roadhog hidoi doraibā
rob: I've been robbed gōtō des
rock iwa
   whisky on the rocks onzarok-ku
roll *(bread)* rōru bred-do
Roman Catholic rōma katorik-ku
romantic romanchik-ku (na)
roof yane
room heya
   have you got a single room? hitori-beya ga
  arimas-ka?
   for one night/for three nights ip-paku/
  sampaku
  YOU MAY THEN HEAR...
  washitsu ni shimas-ka, yōshitsu ni shimas-
  ka? *Japanese- or Western-style?*
  manshitsu des *sorry, we're full*

room service rūmu sābisu
rope rōpu
rose bara
rough *(person)* ki no arai
   (sea) areta
roughly *(approximately)* oyoso
round *(circular)* marui
round-trip: a round-trip ticket to . . . . . . made
  no ōfku
roundabout rōtarī
route rūto
  which is the prettiest/fastest route? ichiban
  kirei na/hayai rūto wa dore des-ka?
rowboat bōto
rubber *(material)* gomu
  (eraser) keshigomu
rubber band wagomu
rudder kaji
rude busahō (na)
ruin haikyo
rum ramshu
  rum and Coke ramshu to kōku
run: hurry, run! isoide!
  I've run out of gas/money gasorin/o-kane ga
  nakunari-mashta
sad kanashī
safe anzen (na)
  will it be safe? anzen des-ka?
  is it safe to swim here? koko de oyogu no wa
  anzen des-ka?
safety anzen
safety pin anzempin
sailor funanori
sake cup sakazuki
salad sarada
salami sarami
sale: is it for sale? urimono des-ka?
salesclerk tenin
sales counter kaikei
salmon sake

salt shio
same onaji
  the same again, please onaji no o mō hitotsu
  kudasai
  the same to you anata mo
sand suna
sandal sandaru
sandwich sandoit-chi
sanitary napkin seiriyō napkin
satisfactory manzoku (na)
Saturday do-yōbi
sauce *(Japanese)* shōyu
  (Western) sōs
saucepan nabe
saucer ukezara
sausage sōsēji
save *(life)* taskemas
say: how do you say . . . in Japanese? Nihon-
  go de . . . o dō īmas-ka?
  what did he say? non to īmashta-ka?
scarf skāfu
scenery keshki
schedule skejūru
  on/behind schedule skejūru-dōri/skejūru-yori
  osoi
scheduled flight teikibin
school gak-kō
scissors hasami
scooter skūtā
Scotland Skot-torando
Scottish Skot-torando (no)
  I'm Scottish Skot-torando-jin des
scratch *(noun)* kizu
scream *(verb)* sakebimas
screw *(noun)* neji
screwdriver nejimawashi
sea umi
  by the sea umibe ni
seafood kaisan shokuhin
seal: personal seal hanko
search *(verb)* sagashimas

search party sōsakutai
seasick: I get seasick funa-yoi shimas
  I feel seasick funa-yoi des
seaside umibe
let's go to the seaside umibe e ikimashō
season kisetsu
  in the high season kisetsu no sakari ni
  in the low season kisetsu hazure ni
seasoning chōmiryō
seat seki
  is this somebody's seat? dareka imas-ka?
seat belt shīto beruto
sea urchin uni
seaweed kaisō
second (*adjective*) nibam-me (no)
  (*time*) byō
  just a second chot-to mat-te kudasai
secondhand sekohan
see mimas
  oh, I see ā sō des-ka
  have you seen...? ...o mimashta-ka?
  can I see the room? heya o misete kudasai
seem: it seems to sono yō des
seldom met-ta ni...-masen
  it seldom works met-ta ni hatarakimasen
self-service serufu sābisu
sell urimas
send okurimas
sensitive binkan (na)
sentimental kanshōteki (na)
separate (*adjective*) betsu-betsu (no)
  I'm separated bek-kyochū des
  can we pay separately? betsu-betsu ni
  haraemas-ka?
September ku-gatsu
serious majime (na)
  I'm serious majime des yo
  this is serious kore wa jūdai des
  is it serious, doctor? hidoi des-ka sensei?
service: the service was excellent/poor sābisu
  wa yokat-ta/yokunakat-ta des

....

service station gasorin stando
several ikutska (no)
sexy sekshī (na)
shade: in the shade kage ni
shake furimas
  to shake hands akshu o shimas
» *TRAVEL TIP: Japanese bow to each other without*
  shaking hands, but they will offer to shake
  yours as a Westerner
shallow asai
shame: what a shame! o-kinodoku ni!
shampoo shampū
share: to share a room/table ish-sho ni
  heya/tēburu o tskaimas
shark same
sharp surudoi
shave sorimas
shaver shēbā
shaving cream shēbing-gu fōmu
she kanojo
  she is American Amerika-jin des
  she has left demashta
sheep hitsuji
sheet *(linen)* shītsu
  you haven't changed my sheets shītsu o
  kaemasen deshta ne
shelf tana
shell kaigara
shellfish kai
sherry sherī
Shinto Shintō
ship fune
shirt shatsu
shock *(noun)* shok-ku
  I got an electric shock from the . . . . . . de
  kanden shimashta
shock absorber shok-ku abusōbā
shoe kutsu
» *TRAVEL TIP: shoe sizes*

US	6	6½	7	7½	8	8½
Japan	23	23½	24	24½	25	25½

» *TRAVEL TIP: if you are invited to a Japanese home, remove your shoes at the entrance*
shop mise
 I've some shopping to do kaimono o shimas
shore kishi
short *(person)* se no hikui
 (vacation) mijikai
 I'm three short mit-tsu tarimasen
shortcut chikamichi
shorts hanzubon
shoulder kata
shout *(verb)* sakebimas
show: please show me misete kudasai
shower: with shower shawātski (no)
shrimp kuruma-ebi
shrine *(Shinto)* jinja
shut: it was shut shimat-te imashta
 shut up! damare!
shy hazkashi-gari (no)
sick *(ill)* byōki (no)
 I feel sick kimochi ga warui des
 he's been sick *(has vomited)* hakimashta
side *(of building, etc.)* yoko
 by the side of the road dōro no waki de
side street wakimichi
sidewalk hodō
sight: it's out of sight miemasen
sight-seeing tour kankō ryokō
 we'd like to go on a sight-seeing tour kankō ryokō ni ikitai des
sign *(notice)* sain
signal: he didn't signal *(driver)* aizu o dashimasen deshta
signature shomei
» *TRAVEL TIP: Japanese use seals (called "hanko") instead of signatures for signing official documents; Japanese also learn to sign their name in romanized form*
silence shizukesa
silk kinu

....

silly baka (na)
» *TRAVEL TIP: this word can be used with reference to yourself, but avoid using it for other people; see* **idiot**
silver gin
similar dōyō (no)
simple kantan (na)
since: since last week senshū kara
  since we arrived *(from that time)* tsuite irai
  (because) . . . node
sincere seijitsu (na)
  yours sincerely keigu
sing utaimas
single *(item)* hitotsu (no)
  (person) hitori (no)
  single room hitori-beya
  I'm single hitori des
sink: it sank shizumimashta
sister *(own) (older)* ane
  (younger) imōto
  (someone else's) (older) o-nē-san
  (younger) imōto-san
sit: can I sit here? koko ni suwat-te mo ī des-ka?
size saizu
skid *(verb)* yokosuberi shimas
skin hifu
skirt skāto
sky sora
sleep: I can't sleep nemuremasen
  YOU MAY HEAR. . .
  yoku nemurimashta-ka? *did you sleep well?*
sleeper *(rail)* shindaisha
sleeping bag nebukuro
sleeping pill suimin-yaku
sleeve sode
slide *(photographic)* suraido
sliding door fusuma
slippers surip-pa
slow *(train, etc.)* noroi
  (speech, etc.) yuk-kuri

could you speak a little slower? mō skoshi
yuk-kuri hanashte kudasai
small chīsai
small change komakai o-kane
smell: there's a funny smell hen-na nioi ga
shimas
　it smells nioimas
smile *(verb)* hoho-emimas
smoke *(noun)* kemuri
　do you smoke? tabako o suimas-ka?
　can I smoke? tabako o sut-te mo ī des-ka?
　I don't smoke suimasen
smooth nameraka (na)
snack: can we just have a snack? karui
shokuji ga dekimas-ka?
snow yuki
so: it's so hot today kyō was totemo atsui des
　not so much amari taksan ja naku
　so-so mā-mā
soap sek-ken
sober yot-te inai
sock kutsushta
soda (water) sōdasui
soft drink softo-dorinku
sole *(of foot)* ashi no ura
　(of shoe) kutsu no soko-gawa
　(fish) shtabirame
　could you put new soles on these? kutsu no
soko o harikaete kudasai
　YOU MAY THEN HEAR...
　kawa des-ka? gomu des-ka? *leather or rubber?*
some: some people aru hitobito
　can I have some? skoshi kudasai
　can I have some grapes/some bread?
budō/pan o kudasai
　can I have some more? mō skoshi kudasai
somebody dare ka
something nani ka
sometime itsu ka
sometimes tokidoki
somewhere doko ka

son *(own)* musko
  (someone else's) musko-san
song uta
soon mamonaku
  as soon as possible dekiru dake hayaku
  sooner mot-to hayaku
sore: it's sore itai des
  I have a sore throat nodo ga itai
sorry: (I'm) sorry sumimasen
» *TRAVEL TIP: apologies are profusely offered to*
  people with whom you have some form of
  personal relationship, but the rules don't
  always apply to strangers; for example, don't
  expect an apology if someone bumps into you
  on the street
sort: this sort kono yō na
  will you sort it out? umaku tori-hakarat-te
  kudasai
soup *(Japanese)* shiru-mono
  (Western) sūpu
sour sup-pai
south minami
South Africa Minami Afurika
South African Minami Afurika-jin
souvenir o-miyage
spade shaberu
spare: spare part yobi no buhin
  spare wheel yobi no taiya
spark plug spāku puragu
speak: do you speak English? Eigo o
  hanashimas-ka?
  I don't speak . . . . . . o hanashimasen
special tokubetsu (na)
specialist sem-monka
specially toku ni
speed spīdo
  he was speeding kare wa spīdo ihan deshta
speed limit sokudo seigen
speedometer sokudo no mētā
spend *(money)* tsukaimas
spice chōmiryō

is it spicy? karai des-ka?
spider kumo
spirits *(drink)* arukōru
spoon spūn
sprain: I've sprained my... ...o
kujikimashta
spring *(of car, seat)* spuring-gu
(season) haru
square *(in town)* hiroba
2 square miles ni-mairu shihō
stairs kaidan
stale *(food)* aji no kawat-ta
stalls ik-kai zempō no it-tōseki
stamp kit-te
two stamps for America Amerika-yuki no
kit-te ni-mai
standard *(adjective)* hyōjin (no)
star hoshi
start *(noun)* stāto
(verb) hajimarimas
my car won't start kuruma ga hashiranai
deshō
when does it start? itsu hajimarimas-ka?
starter *(of car)* shidōki
(food) zensai
starving: I'm starving onaka ga peko-peko
des
station eki
statue zō
stay: we enjoyed our stay taizai o tanoshimi-
mashta
stay there soko ni ite kudasai
I'm staying at Hotel... ...hoteru ni tomat-
te imas
steak stēki
YOU MAY HEAR...
stēki wa dono yō ni shimas-ka? *how would you
like your steak?*
nama-yake des-ka? *rare?*
futsū des-ka? *medium?*
yoku yakimas-ka? *well done?*

» *TRAVEL TIP: steak is a luxury in Japan due to a complicated distribution system where numerous middlemen take their financial cut*

steep kyū (na)

steering stearing-gu

steering wheel kuruma no handoru

step *(noun)* dan

stereo stereo

stewardess schuādes

sticky beto-beto (no)

stiff katai

still: keep still! ugokanaide kudasai!

  I'm still here mada koko ni imas

stink *(noun)* akushū

stolen: my wallet's been stolen saifu ga nusumare-mashta

stomach onaka

  I have a stomachache onaka go itai des

  have you got something for an upset stomach? iniyoi kusuri ga arimas-ka?

stone ishi

stop: stop! tomat-te!

  (overnight) shukuhaku

  do you stop near...? ...no chikaku de tomarimas-ka?

stopover: can we make a stopover in Osaka? Ōsaka ni tochūgesha dekimas-ka?

storm arashi

stove renji

straight mas-sugu

  go straight on mas-sugu it-te kudasai

  straight whisky storēto

strange *(odd)* hen (na)

  (unknown) mita koto no nai

stranger mishiranu hito

  I'm a stranger here koko wa hajimete des

strawberry ichigo

street tōri

string himo

stroke: he's had a stroke sot-chū no hos-sa des

stroller kuruma-isu

strong *(person, material, drink)* tsuyoi
student gaksei
stung: I've been stung sasaremashta
stupid baka (na)
» *TRAVEL TIP: see* **silly**
subway chikatetsu
» *TRAVEL TIP: underground trains, like buses, are*
   frequent and reliable, but have their
   destination displayed only in Japanese writing;
   try to avoid traveling during the rush hour
such: such a lot konna ni taksan
suddenly totsuzen
sugar satō
suit *(man's, woman's)* sūtsu
suitable tekitō (na)
suitcase sūtsukēsu
summer natsu
summer kimono yukata
sun taiyō
   in the sun hinata de
   out of the sun hikage de
sunbathing nik-kō-yoku
sunblock hiyakedome
sunburn yakedo
Sunday nichi-yōbi
» *TRAVEL TIP: while banks and government offices*
   are closed on Sundays, it is a major day for
   shops and department stores, which are closed
   on another day of the week
sunglasses san-guras
sunstroke nish-shabyō
suntan oil santan oiru
supermarket sūpā
sure: I'm not sure tashka de-wa arimasen
   are you sure? tashka des-ka?
   sure! mochiron!
surname myōji
» *TRAVEL TIP: surname plus "-san" is the standard*
   way of addressing a Japanese; see also **first**
   name
swearword warui kotoba

sweat *(verb)* ase o kakimas
  (noun) ase
sweater sētā
sweet: it's too sweet ama-sugimas
  (dessert) dezāto
swerve: I had to swerve kyū ni hōkō o kae-
  nakereba narimasen deshta
swim: I'm going for a swim oyogi ni ikimas
  let's go for a swim oyogi ni ikimashō
swimming suit mizugi
switch *(noun)* suit-chi
  to switch on/off tskemas/keshimas
table tēburu
  a table for four yon-nin yō no tēburu
Taiwan Taiwan
take torimas
  can I take this (with me)? mot-te it-te mo ī
  des-ka?
  will you take me to the airport? kūkō made
  tsurete it-te kudasai
  how long will it take? dono kurai
  kakarimas-ka?
  somebody has taken my bags dare ka ga
  bag-gu o nusumimashta
  can I take you out tonight? komban
  go-shōkai shte ī des-ka?
talcum powder tarukamu paudā
talk *(verb)* hanashimas
tall *(person)* se ga takai
  (building) takai
tampons tampon
tan *(noun)* hiyake
  I want to get a tan hiyake shtai des
tank *(of car)* nenryō tanku
tape *(for cassette)* tēpu
  (sticky) serotēpu
tape recorder tēpu rekōdā
tariff *(list of charges)* ryōkinhyō
taste *(noun)* aji
  can I taste it? ajimi shte ī des-ka?
  it tastes horrible mazui des

it tastes very nice oichī des

taxi takshī

will you get me a taxi? takshī o yonde kudasai

where can I get a taxi? doko de takshī ni noremas-ka?

» *TRAVEL TIP: although expensive, taxis are metered and there is no tipping; late at night the price increases, but this is shown on the meter; beware of the rear door on the left-hand side, which opens and closes automatically*

taxi driver takshī doraibā

tea *(Japanese-style)* o-cha
(Western-style) kōcha

could I have a cup of tea? kōcha ip-pai kudasai

could I have a pot of tea? kōcha o pot-to de kudasai

with milk/lemon miruku/remon de

» *TRAVEL TIP: while Japanese tea (o-cha) is served everywhere and all day (but never with sugar or lemon or milk!), Western-style tea (kōcha) is more prestigious and thus more expensive; in a coffee shop you wouldn't order Japanese-style tea*

tea ceremony chano-yu

teach: could you teach me? oshiete kudasai

could you teach me...? ...o oshiete kudasai

teacher sensei

tea house chamise

telegram dempō

I want to send a telegram dempō o uchitai des

telephone *(noun)* denwa

can I make a phone call? denwa o kakete mo ī des-ka?

can I speak to Kazue? Kazue-san to o-hanashi dekimas-ka?

could you get the number for me? ban-go o mitsukete kudasai

I'll phone you denwa shimas
   telephone directory denwa-chō
   telephone booth kōshū denwa
» *TRAVEL TIP: there are public phones everywhere
in Japan; many can be operated with coins and
with a phonecard (terefon kādo), so it is worth
getting one by asking a Japanese to point out a
phonecard vending machine (in train stations
and sometimes beside public phones)*
   YOU MAY HEAR…
   moshi-moshi *hello*
television terebi
   I'd like to watch some television terebi o
   mitai des
tell: could you tell me where…? …wa doko
   ka oshiete kudasai
temperature *(weather)* kion
   (body) taion
   (water) suion
temple *(Buddhist)* o-tera
tennis tenis
tennis ball tenis bōru
tennis court tenis kōto
tennis racket tenis raket-to
tent tento
terminal shūten
terrible totemo hidoi
terrific sugoi
than yori
   bigger than… …yori ōkī des
thanks, thank you arigatō, arigatō gozaimas
   no, thank you īe, kek-kō des
   thank you very much dōmo arigatō
   gozaimas
   thank you for your help taskete kudasat-te
   arigatō
   YOU MAY THEN HEAR…
   dō itashimashte! *you're welcome!*
» *TRAVEL TIP: the word "sumimasen," which
means "sorry," is also often used to say thank
you, the implication being that the granting of*

*a favor, however trifling, has caused some upset
in the other's life*

that *(pronoun)* sore
   (adjective) sono
   (further away: pronoun) are
   (further away: adjective) ano
   that man/that table sono hito/tēburu
   I would like that one sore o kudasai
   how do you say that? dō īmas-ka?
   I think that . . . . . . da to omoimas

the *Japanese has no word for "the"*

theatre gekijō

their karera no
   it's their bag karera no bag-gu des
   it's theirs karera no des

them *(people)* karera o
   (things) sorera o
   with them *(people)* karera to ish-sho ni
   (things) sorera to ish-sho ni
   who?—them dare des-ka?—karera des

then *(at that time)* sono toki
   (after that) sorekara

there soko de
   how do I get there? dō yat-te soko ni
   ikimas-ka?
   is there/are there . . . ? *(things)* . . . ga arimas-ka?
   (people) . . . ga imas-ka?
   there is/there are . . . *(things)* . . . ga arimas
   (people) . . . ga imas
   there isn't/there aren't . . .
   (things) . . . ga arimasen
   (people) . . . ga imasen
   there you are *(giving something)* dōzo

thermos bottle mahōbin

these *(pronoun)* korera
   these apples/these people kono rin-go/kono
   hito
   can I take these? kore o tot-te ī des-ka?

they karera
   they are friends of mine watashi no
   tomodachi des

thick *(wood)* atsui
  (soup) koi
thief dorobō
thigh momo
thin *(body)* hosoi
  (paper) usui
thing mono
  I've lost all my things zembu no mono o
  nakushimashta
think kan-gaemas
  I'll think it over kan-gaete mimas
  I think so sō da to omoimas
  I don't think so sō da to omoimasen
third *(adjective)* sambam-me (no)
thirsty nodo no kawaita
  I'm thirsty nodo ga kawakimashta
this *(pronoun)* kore
  this hotel/this street kono hoteru/kono tōri
  can I have this one? kore o kudasai
  this is my wife kore wa tsuma des
  this is Mr.... kochira wa...-san des
  is this...? kore wa...des-ka?
those *(pronoun)* arera
  those... arera no...
  no, not these, those! ie, korera ja nakute,
  arera des!
thread *(noun)* ito
throat nodo
throttle *(motorbike)* surot-toru
through: through Nagasaki Nagasaki o tōt-te
throw *(verb)* nagemas
thumb oya-yubi
thumbtack gabyō
thunder *(noun)* kaminari
thunderstorm raiu
Thursday moku-yōbi
ticket kip-pu
  ticket office kip-pu uriba
tie *(necktie)* nektai
tight *(clothes)* kitsui
tights taitsu

time jikan
>> **what time is it?** nanji des-ka?
>> **I haven't got time** jikan ga arimasen
>> **for the time being** sashiatari
>> **this time/last time/next time**
>> konkai/senkai/jikai
>> **3 times** sankai
>> **have a good time!** tanoshiku sugoshte
>> kudasai!

» *TRAVEL TIP: how to tell the time; key words are
"fun" (minutes) which can change to "pun"; "ji"
(hours); "sugi" (past); "mae" (to); "-han" added
to the hour means "half"*
>> **it's one o'clock** ichiji des
>> **it's two/three/four/five/six o'clock**
>> niji/sanji/yoji/goji/rokuji des
>> **it's 5/10/20/25 past seven** shichiji gofun/
>> jup-pun/nijup-pun/nijū-gofun sugi des
>> **it's quarter past eight/eight fifteen** hachiji
>> jūgofun sugi des
>> **it's half past nine/nine thirty** kujihan des
>> **it's 25/20/10/5 to ten** jūji nijū-gofun/nijup-
>> pun/jup-pun/gofun mae des
>> **it's quarter to eleven/10:45** jūichiji jūgofun
>> mae des/jūji yonjū-gofun des
>> **at twelve o'clock** jūniji ni

timetable jikanhyō
tip (noun) chip-pu
» *TRAVEL TIP: there's no tipping in Japan, except
in hotels that are used to having a lot of
Western customers*
tire taiya
>> **I need a new tire** atarashī taiya ga irimas

» *TRAVEL TIP: tire pressures*

lb/sq. in.	18	20	22	26	28	30
kg/sq. cm	1.3	1.4	1.5	1.8	2	2.1

tired tskareta
>> **I'm tired** tskarete imas
tissues tish-shū
to: to Hiroshima/to America Hiroshima e/
Amerika e

toast *(bread)* tōsto
   (drinking) kampai
tobacco tabako
tobacco shop tabako-ya
today kyō
toe tsumasaki
together ish-sho (ni)
   we're together ish-sho des
   can we pay all together? zembu is-sho ni haraemas-ka?
toilet o-tearai
   where are the toilets? o-tearai wa doko des-ka?
   I have to go to the toilet o-tearai ni ikitai des
   there's no toilet paper toiret-to pēpā ga arimasen
   ladies' rest room fujin-yō toire
   men's rest room otoko no hito-tachi
» *TRAVEL TIP: squat toilets are frequent in Japan (except in Western-style hotels); while toilet paper is usually provided, towels aren't, so it's advisable to develop the habit of carrying hand-kerchiefs or paper napkins for drying your hands*
   toilet *(public)* kōshū benjo
» *TRAVEL TIP: large department stores in cities are your best bet; in coffee shops, it may be worth paying for a cup of coffee, etc. to use their toilet facilities; or you could try your luck by asking politely: toire o tsukat-te mo ī des-ka?—may I use the toilet?; train stations do have public toilets, but mostly beyond the ticket barrier; you may have to buy at least a platform ticket (nyūjō-ken) to reach them*
tomato tomato
tomato juice tomato jūsu
tomorrow ashta
   tomorrow morning/afternoon/evening ashta no asa/no gogo/no ban
   the day after tomorrow asat-te
   see you tomorrow ja mata ashta
ton Ei-ton

» *TRAVEL TIP: 1 ton = 1,016 kilos*
tongue shta
tonic (water) tonik-ku
tonight komban
tonsillitis hentōsen-en
too *(also)* mo
   that's too much ō-sugimas
   (too expensive) taka-sugimas
   not too fast please amari hayaku naku
   onegai shimas
tool dōgu
tooth ha
   I've got a toothache ha ga itai des
toothbrush haburashi
toothpaste neri-hamigaki
top: on top of . . . . . . no ue ni
   on the top floor saijōkai ni
   at the top tep-pen ni
total *(noun)* gōkei
tough *(meat)* katai
tour *(noun)* tsuā
   we'd like to go on a tour of the town machi
   no tsuā ni ikitai des
   package tour pak-kēji tsuā
tourist ryokōsha
   I'm a tourist ryokōsha des
tourist office ryokōsha an-naijo
tow *(verb)* hikimas
   can you give me a tow? hīte kudasai
towards . . . . . . no hō e
   he was coming straight towards me
   watashi no hō e mas-sugu kimashta
towel taoru
town machi
   in town machi de
   would you take me into the town? machi ni
   tsurete it-te kudasai
towrope hikizuna
traditional dentōteki (na)
   a traditional Japanese meal dentōteki na
   Nihon no shokuji

traffic kōtsū
traffic lights shin-gō
train densha
  bullet train shinkan-sen
  also see **subway**
» *TRAVEL TIP: very punctual, but also very*
  expensive; try to buy a Japan Rail Pass from a
  travel agency before you visit Japan; station
  signs are written both in Japanese and in
  romanized writing
tranquilizers torankiraizā
translate hon-yaku shimas
  would you translate that for me? sore o
  hon-yaku shte kudasai
translator hon-yaksha
transmission *(of car)* toransmish-shon
travel: we're traveling around tsuā o shte imas
travel agency ryokōgaisha
traveler's check toraberāzu chek-ku
tree ki
tremendous monosugoi
trim: just a trim, please soroete kudasai
trip *(noun)* ryokō
  we want to go on a trip to... ...e ryokō
  shtai des
  have a good trip! dōzo go-buji de!
trouble *(noun)* shimpai
  I'm having trouble with the steering/my
  back stearing-gu/senaka ga shimpai des
trousers zubon
trout masu
truck torak-ku
truck driver torak-ku doraibā
true hontō (no)
  it's not true hontō de-wa arimasen
trunk *(car)* kurumano toranku
trunks *(swimming)* suiei pantsu
try *(verb)* shte mimas
  can I try? yat-te mo ī des-ka?
  please try dōzo tameshte mite kudasai
  can I try it on? kite mo ī des-ka?

T-shirt tī shatsu
Tuesday ka-yōbi
Turkish bath sōpurando
turn: where do we turn off? doko de
  magarimas-ka?
  he turned without indicating shiji nashi ni
  magarimashta
twice nikai
  twice as much nibai
twin beds tsuin bed-do
typewriter taipuraitā
typhoon taifū
typical tenkeiteki (na)
ugly minikui
ulcer kaiyō
umbrella kasa
uncle *(own)* oji
  (someone else's) oji-san
uncomfortable *(furniture, etc.)* kokochi no
  yoku nai
unconscious muishki (na)
under... ...no shta ni
underdone nama-yake (no)
understand: I understand wakarimas
  I don't understand wakarimasen
  do you understand? wakarimas-ka?
underwear *(shorts)* pants
undo *(clothes, etc.)* nugimas
unfriendly yoso-yososhī
unhappy kanashī
United States Gash-shūkoku
unleaded gas mu-en gasorin
unlock kagi o akemas
until... ...made
  until next year rainen made
unusual kawat-ta
up ue (ni)
  up there asoko no ue
  it's up there asoko no ue ni arimas
  he's not up yet *(out of bed)* mada okite
  imasen

what's up? nani ka arimashta-ka?
upside-down sakasama
upstairs ue
urgent kinkyū (na)
us watashi-tachi
use: can I use...? ...o tsukat-te mo ī des-ka?
useful yaku ni tatsu
usual futsū (no)
  as usual itsumo no tōri ni
usually futsū wa
U-turn yūtān
vacancy: do you have any vacancies?
  (hotel) aita heya ga arimas-ka?
vacate *(room)* kara ni shimas
vacation kyūka
  I'm on vacation kyūka des
vaccination yobōchūsha
valid yūkō (na)
  how long is it valid for? dono kurai yūkō
  des-ka?
valuable kachi no aru
  will you look after my valuables? kichōhin
  o mite ite kudasai
value kachi
valve barubu
van ban
vanilla banira
varicose veins jōmyaku ryū
veal ko-ushi no niku
vegetables yasai
vegetarian saishoku-shugi-sha
ventilator kanki-sen
very totemo
  very much totemo
via... ...o tōt-te
video camera bideo kamera
village mura
vinegar su
violent hageshī
visibility shikai
visit *(verb)* tazunemas

vodka uok-ka
voice koe
volcano kazan
voltage denatsu
» *TRAVEL TIP: voltage is 100; see* **electricity**
waist uesto
» *TRAVEL TIP: waist measurements*

US	24	26	28	30	32	34	36
Japan	61	66	71	76	80	87	91

wait: will we have to wait long? nagaku mata-
nakereba narimasen-ka?
  wait for me mat-te kudasai
  I'm waiting for a friend/my wife
  tomodachi/tsuma o mat-te imas
waiter uētā
  waiter! chot-to onegai shimas
waitress uētoresu
  waitress! chot-to onegai shimas
wake: will you wake me up at 7:30?
shichiji-han ni okoshte kudasai
Wales Uēruz
walk: can we walk there? asoko e
arukimashō-ka?
  **are there any good walks around
  here?** kono atari ni yoi sampomichi ga
  arimas-ka?
walking shoes haiking-gu-shūzu
wall kabe
wallet saifu
want: I want/she wants a . . . . . . ga hoshī des
  I want to talk to the consul ryōji to
  hanashtai des
  what do you want? nani go hoshī des-ka?
  I don't want to sō shtaku arimasen
  he wants/I want to . . . . . . -tai des
warm atatakai
warning chūi
was: I was/he was/it was . . . . . . deshta
wash: can you wash these for me? kore o
arat-te kudasai
  where can I wash? doko de araemas-ka?

....

washer *(for nut)* wash-shā
wasp hachi
watch *(wrist-)* tokei
  will you watch my bags for me? bag-gu o
  mite ite kudasai
  watch out! abunai!
water mizu
  could I have some water? o-mizu o kudasai
waterproof bōsui (no)
waterskiing suijōskī
way: we'd like to eat the Japanese way
  Nihon-shiki de tabetai des
  could you tell me the way to ...? ... e dō
  ikimas-ka?
  see **where** *for answers*
  no way! dame des!
we watashi-tachi
  we are American Amerika-jin des
weak *(person, drink)* yowai
weather tenki
  what awful weather! hidoi tenki des ne!
  what's the weather forecast? tenkiyohō wa
  dō des-ka?
  YOU MAY THEN HEAR ...
  ame ga furu deshō *it may rain*
  hareru deshō *it may be fine*
  haretari kumot-tari deshō *it may be fine, but*
  occasionally cloudy
  samuku naru deshō *it may become cold*
  atsuku naru deshō *it may become hot*
Wednesday sui-yōbi
week shū
  a week today/tomorrow ish-shūkan-go no
  kyō/ashta
  on the weekend shūmatsu ni
weight omosa
well: I'm not feeling well kibun ga yoku
  arimasen
  how are you?–very well, thanks o-genki
  des-ka?–hai, okagesama de genki des

you speak English very well Eigo ga totemo jōzu des ne

Welsh Uērez (no)

were: you/we/they were… …deshta

west nishi

   the West Seiyō

Westerner Seiyō-jin

Western-style yōfū

West Indies Nishi Indo shotō

wet nureta

whale kujira

what: what is that? sore wa nan des-ka?

   what for? nan no tame des-ka?

what? ē?

wheel sharin

wheelchair kuruma-isu

when? itsu?

   when is breakfast? chōshoku wa itsu des-ka?

   when we arrived tsuita toki

where? doko des-ka?

   where is the post office? yūbinkyoku wa doko des-ka?

YOU MAY THEN HEAR…

mas-sugu *straight ahead*

migi ni magat-te *turn right*

hidari ni magat-te *turn left*

hoka no hōkō des *it's in the other direction*

migi/hidari no nibam-me *second on the right/left*

which: which bus? dono bas des-ka?

   which (one)? dore des-ka?

whisky uiskī

white shiroi

white-collar worker sararī-man

who? dare des-ka?

whose? dare no des-ka?

   whose is this? kore wa dare no des-ka?

why? naze des-ka?

   why not? dōshte des-ka?

   ok, why not? ē, mochiron des

....

wide hiroi
wife *(own)* tsuma
   (someone else's) oku-san
will: when will it finish? itsu owarimas-ka?
   will you do it? sore o shimas-ka?
   I will come back modorimas
window mado
   near the window mado no soba ni
windshield furonto garasu
windshield wipers furonto garasu no waipā
windy kaze no aru
wine wain
   can I see the wine list? wainristo o misete
kudasai
» *TRAVEL TIP: although Japan does produce some*
   wines (e.g., Suntory), most wines are imported
   and therefore expensive; restaurants serving
   only Japanese food will rarely serve wine
winter fuyu
wire harigane
   (electric) densen
wish: best wishes! go-seikō o!
with . . . . . . to ish-sho ni
   with me watashi to ish-sho ni
without . . . . . . nashi de
   without sugar satō nashi de
witness shōnin
woman/women josei
wonderful subarashī
won't: it won't start stāto shimasen
wood ki
wool yōmō
word kotoba
   I don't know that word sono kotoba o
shirimasen
work *(verb)* hatarakimas
   (noun) shigoto
   it's not working sadō shte imasen
   I work/she works in America Amerika de
hatarakimas
worry *(noun)* shimpai

I'm worried about him kare ga shimpai des
  don't worry shimpai shinaide kudasai
worse: it's worse mae yori warui des
  he's getting worse waruku nat-te imas
worst saiaku (no)
wrap: could you wrap it up? kore o tsutsunde
  kudasai
wrench *(tool)* renchi
wrist tekubi
write kakimas
  could you write it down? sore o kaite
  kudasai
  I'll write to you tegami o kakimas
writing: Japanese writing Nihon-go no
  kakikata
writing paper binsen
wrong machigai
  I think the bill's wrong kanjō ga machigai
  da to omoimas
  there's something wrong with... ...wa
  nani ka okashī des
  you're wrong machigat-te imas
  sorry, wrong number sumimasen, ban-gō o
  machigae-mashta
X-ray rentogen shashin
yacht yot-to
yard
» *TRAVEL TIP: 1 yard = 91.44 cm = 0.91 m*
year toshi
  this year/next year kotoshi/rainen
yellow kīroi
yen en
yes hai
yesterday kinō
  the day before yesterday ototoi
  yesterday morning/yesterday afternoon
  kinō no asa/kinō no gogo
yet: is it ready yet? mada des-ka?
  not yet mada des
yogurt yōguruto
yogurt drink yōguruto dorinku

you *(singular)* anata
 (plural) anatatachi
 I like you anata ga ski des
 with you anata to ish-sho ni
» *TRAVEL TIP: it is not common to address*
 Japanese with the direct translation of you
 "anata"; instead, use the family name and
 "-san" (for both sexes), or first name and "-san"
 if you are good friends; children up to their
 teens can be addressed by their first name and
 "-chan"
young wakai
your *(singular)* anata no
 (plural) anatatachi no
 is this your camera? anata no kamera
 des-ka?
 is this yours? anata no des-ka?
youth hostel yūs hosteru
Zen Buddhism Zen
zero zero
 below zero zero ika
zip fasnā

Japanese signs and notices

空	aki *free, vacant*
アメリカ	Amerika *America*
案内所	an-naijo *information*
バー	bā *bar*
バーゲン	bāgen *bargain(s)*
バスのりば	bas noriba *bus stop*
バス停	bastei *bus stop*
米国	Beikoku *USA*
美術館	bijutsukan *art gallery*
病院	byōin *hospital*
地下鉄	chikatetsu *subway*
駐車禁止	chūsha kinshi *no parking*
男子用	danshiyō *men's room*
出口	deguchi *exit*
電話	denwa *telephone*
電話番号	denwa ban-gō *telephone number*

デパート	depāto *department store*
土曜日	do-yōbi *Saturday*
どうぞ…	dōzo *please*
映画館	eigakan *movie theater*
英国	Eikoku *United Kingdom*
駅前	ekimae *in front of the station*
円	en *Yen*
エレベーター	erebētā *elevator*
フロント	fronto *reception (desk)*
外国人	gaikoku-jin *foreign nationals*
月曜日	getsu-yōbi *Monday*
銀行	ginkō *bank*
グリーン車	gurīn-sha *'green car' — first class*
博物館	hakubutskan *museum*
閉	hei *close*
左	hidari *left*

東	higashi *east*
非常電話	hijō denwa *emergency telephone*
非常口	hijōguchi *emergency exit*
引く	hiku *pull*
開く	hiraku *open*
ホステス バー	hostes bā *hostess bar*
ホテル	hoteru *hotel*
110番	hyaku-tōban *110 (for police)*
イギリス	Igirisu *United Kingdom*
入口	iriguchi *entrance*
…人	. . . jin *person*
徐行	jokō *slow*
女子用	joshiyō *ladies' room*
住所	jūsho *address*
開	kai *open*
回送	kaisō *not in service*

カナダ	Kanada *Canada*
火災報知器	kasai hōchiki *fire alarm*
為替レート	kawase rēto *exchange rate*
火曜日	ka-yōbi *Tuesday*
県	ken *prefecture*
危険	kiken *danger*
禁煙	kin-en *no smoking*
禁止します	kinshi shimas *forbidden*
金曜日	kin-yōbi *Friday*
切符売り場	kip-pu uriba *ticket office*
北	kita *north*
切手	kit-te *stamps*
コインロッカー	koin-rok-kā *luggage lockers*
航空	kōkū *airline*
航空便	kōkūbin *airmail*
故障	koshō *out of order*

空港	kūkō *airport*
クリーニング	kurīning-gu *dry cleaning*
薬屋	kusuriya *pharmacy*
京都	Kyōto *Kyoto*
急カーブ	kyū kābu *sharp bend*
急行	kyūko *express train*
救急箱	kyūkyūbako *first aid box*
窓口	madoguchi *ticket window*
前売券	mae-uriken *advance reservations*
満席	manseki *all seats taken*
免税店	menzeiten *duty-free shop*
右	migi *right*
南	minami *south*
みやげ店	miyageten *souvenir shop*
木曜日	moku-yōbi *Thursday*
年齢	nenrei *age*

日曜日	nichi-yōbi	*Sunday*
日本	Nihon	*Japan*
日本製	Nihonsei	*made in Japan*
西	nishi	*west*
お風呂	o-furo	*bath*
お手洗	o-tearai	*toilet*
温泉	onsen	*hot spring*
大阪	Ōsaka	*Osaka*
オーストラリア	Ōstoraria	*Australia*
押す	osu	*push*
お立見席	otachimi-seki	*standing room only*
両替所	ryōgaejo	*currency exchange office*
旅館	ryokan	*Japanese-style inn*
旅行者小切手	ryokōsha kogit-te	*traveller's check*
サイン	sain	*signature*
サイズ	saiz	*size*

生年月日	seinen gap-pi *date of birth*
セール	sēru *sale*
写真禁止	shashin kinshi *photography forbidden*
氏名	shimei *full name*
市役所	shiyaksho *city hall*
使用中	shiyōchū *occupied*
消化器	shōkaki *fire extinguisher*
食堂	shokudō *restaurant*
食品	shokuhin *food*
下	shta *down*
指定席	shteiseki *reserved seat*
出発	shup-patsu *departure(s)*
スナックバー	snak-ku bā *snack bar*
ソープランド	sōpurando *Turkish bath*
水曜日	suiyōbi *Wednesday*
立入禁止	tachi-iri kinshi *no entry*

タクシーのりば	takshī noriba *taxi stand*
テレフォン・カード	terefon kādo *phonecard*
到着	tōchaku *arrival(s)*
閉じる	tojiru *closed*
東京	Tōkyō *Tokyo*
特急	tok-kyū *limited stop express*
止まれ	tomare *stop*
図書館	toshokan *library*
次は停車	tsugi wa teisha *stopping at next stop*
上	ue *up*
運賃箱	unchimbako *box for fares*
運賃表	unchinhyō *fare table*
売物	urimono *for sale*
浴室	yokushitsu *bathroom*
予約	yoyaku *reserved*
郵便局	yūbin-kyoku *post office*
…行き	. . . yuki *destination . . .*

Numbers

		Chinese-derived	native Japanese
1	一	ichi	hitotsu
2	二	ni	futatsu
3	三	san	mit-tsu
4	四	shi (*or* yon)	yot-tsu
5	五	go	itsutsu
6	六	roku	mut-tsu
7	七	shichi (*or* nana)	nanatsu
8	八	hachi	yat-tsu
9	九	ku (*or* kyū)	kokonotsu
10	十	jū	tō

11	十一	jū-ichi	19	十九	jū-ku
12	十二	jū-ni	20	二十	ni-jū
13	十三	jū-san	21	二十一	ni-jū-ichi
14	十四	jū-shi	22	二十二	ni-jū-ni
15	十五	jū-go	30	三十	san-jū
16	十六	jū-roku	31	三十一	san-jū-ichi
17	十七	jū-shichi	40	四十	yon-jū
18	十八	jū-hachi	50	五十	go-jū

60	六十	roku-jū	200	二百	ni-hyaku
70	七十	nana-jū	300	三百	san-byaku
80	八十	hachi-jū	1,000	千	sen
90	九十	kyū-jū	2,000	二千	ni-sen
100	百	hyaku	3,000	三千	san-zen
101	百一	hyaku-ichi	5,000	五千	go-sen
156	百五十六	hyaku-go-jū-roku	8,000	八千	has-sen
			10,000	一万	ichi-man

12,345 一万二千三百四十五 ichi-man-ni-sen-byaku-yon-jū-go

100,000 　十万　jū-man

1,000,000 　百万　hyaku-man

The numeral "zero" (0) also occurs when the Japanese use Arabic numerals. It is pronounced "rei" or "zero."

Note that Japanese regard 10,000 as a unit (man). So 100,000 is written 10 man and a million 100 man, etc.

Use Chinese-derived numbers for time and money. Native Japanese numbers (only up to 10) can be used for counting objects, the number word coming after its noun, e.g. "three coffees" is "kōhī mit-tsu."